JEAN-CLAUDE CARRIERE

He is one of France's most renowned contemporary writers and has received the Prix Goncourt for his novel, *La Controverse de Valladolid* (1992).

His extensive theatrical credits include adapting *The Mahabharata* for Peter Brook and *Proof* for David Auburn.

He wrote the screenplays for *The Unbearable Lightness of Being, The Tin Drum, Cyrano de Bergerac,* and many others for directors Jacques Tati, Jean-Luc Godard, Milos Forman and Luis Bunuel...

The Little Black Book was first produced in France as *L'Aide-Mémoire* where it received great critical and public acclaim.

aurora metro press

Founded in 1989 to publish and promote new writing, the press has specialised in new drama and fiction, winning recognition and awards from the industry.

new drama

Lysistrata – the sex strike after Aristophanes, adapted by Germaine Greer and Phil Willmott
ISBN 0-9536757-0-X   £7.99

Under Their Influence by Wayne Buchanan
ISBN 0-9536757-5-0 £6.99

Devotion by Leo Butler
ISBN 0-9542330-4-2 £7.99

Best of the Fest. new plays celebrating 10 years of London New Play Festival ed. Phil Setren
ISBN 0-9515877-8-1 £12.99

Three Plays: Jonathan Moore
ISBN 0-9536757-2-6 £10.95

Mediterranean Plays By Women, ed. Marion Baraitser
ISBN 0-9515877-3-0 £9.95

Eastern Promise, seven plays from Central and Eastern Europe eds. Sian Evans and Cheryl Robson
ISBN 0-9515877-9-X £11.99

Coup de Théâtre Company
and Riverside Studios
present

The Little Black Book

by

Jean-Claude Carrière

translated by Solvène Tiffou

AURORA METRO PRESS

RIVERSIDESTUDIOS

Liberté • Égalité • Fraternité
RÉPUBLIQUE FRANÇAISE

This book is supported by the French Ministry for Foreign Affairs, as part of the Burgess Programme headed for the French Embassy in London by the Institut Français du Royaume Uni.

ISBN 0-9542330-7-7   Printed by Antony Rowe, Eastbourne, UK

Coup de Théâtre Company

Marianne Badrichani and Solvène Tiffou co-founded *Coup de Théâtre* to bring plays from the French repertoire to a British audience. The company aims to stage new writing as well as revivals of classics and adaptations of novels, in new translations.

Marianne Badrichani

Marianne Badrichani started her career in theatre, new media and film production, in both Paris and London. She established Monte Cristo Productions, producing several short films, a feature film and various CD-ROMs between 1994 and 1998. In theatre, she has successfully produced and directed a variety of plays which range from the classical to the contemporary. These include *Les Incertitudes du Désir* by Crébillon Fils, *Conversations après un enterrement* by Yasmina Reza and a musical, *Amer à Boire,* (script and directing). With *Together Alone,* which she co-founded in 1999, she staged in London *Linda Her* by Harry Kondoleon, *The Late* by René de Obaldia and *Over Nothing At All* by Nathalie Sarraute.

Solvène Tiffou

After post-graduate studies in Comparative Literature at the Sorbonne, Solvène worked in publishing (Editions Gallimard; Centre National du Livre) and wrote a play, *'An hour for ever'*. She has taken part in the production of documentary films on Henri Alekan, Wim Wenders and Richard Leacock and directed a short film.
'The Little Black Book' is Solvène's first translation.

BIOGRAPHIES

Susannah Harker trained at the Central School for Speech and Drama.
Theatre includes: *The Browning Version*; *Uncle Vanya* (The Gate and New York); *Tartuffe* (Almeida Theatre); *The Importance of Being Earnest* (Aldwych Theatre); *Coriolanus* (Chichester Festival); *Racing Demon* (National Theatre).
Television includes: *Waking the Dead*; *Murder in Mind; Ultra-Violet; Under the Sun; Pride and Prejudice; House of Cards; Chancer; The Fear.*
Film includes: *Trance* (dir. Joe Ahearne); *Intimacy*; *Dry White Season*; *Crucifier of Blood*; *Surviving Picasso.*

Paul McGann trained at RADA.
Theatre includes: *Sabina* (Bush Theatre); *The Seagull* (Liverpool Playhouse); *Loot* (Ambassadors); *A Lie of The Mind*, *The Genius, Oi for England* (all Royal Court).
Television includes: *Our Mutual Friend; The Hanging Gale; Monocled Mutineer; The One That Got Away; Hornblower.*
Film includes: *The Biographer; Alien 3; Withnail & I; Fairy Tale, A True Story.*

Julie Marabelle trained at Central St Martins College of Art and Design, graduating in June 2002 with a First in BA (Hons) Set and Costume Design.
Work includes: costume design for the London Studio Centre's *Intoto* Contemporary Dance (National Tour-Linbury Studio), set and costume design for *The Life of Galileo* (BAC). More recently Julie was the Art Director for a Video installation. She also works freelance as an art director's assistant on projects for the BBC and TV commercials.

Steve Harper is a co-founder of *Together Alone* Theatre Company, with whom he has directed three plays, and Artistic Director of *Perfect Ambiguity* Theatre Company, a new writing company exploring the nature of violence,(shows at the Union Theatre, the White Bear). They are back at the Union in April with a new award-winning play *Random Acts of Malice* by Alan Fraser.

Other directing/assisting credits include shows for Bold and Saucy, I'm A Camera, Bonobo, The Gate, The King's Head and once again the Union Theatre. He has also published papers on the company Forced Entertainment and been awarded an MA (Distinction) in Theatre Studies.

Steve Miller will shortly be starting work on the third Harry Potter film. Later in the year, he will be co-producing a feature film, *Sunstroke*.

Theatre : *Jesus Christ Superstar, Sweeney Todd, Don Giovanni, Ivan – A Miscarriage of Justice, All's Well That Ends Well, This Happy Breed, The Magic Flute, A View from the Bridge.*

Film : *Harry Potter and the Philosopher's Stone, Harry Potter and the Chamber of Secrets* (both as crew). Television: *The Late Show* (BBC), *Viking Scotland* (BBC, Scotland).

Elizabeth Freeman is currently working as a design apprentice for Mountview Theatre School.

Her design credits include: *The Weavers* (Judy Dench Theatre), *Good Person of Sichuan, Rosencrantz and Guildenstern Are Dead, The Appearance of Impropriety*, and *Crave* (Butler University Theatre, Indianapolis).

With many thanks to:

Géraldine D'Amico, Jean-Claude Carrière, Melissa Caron,
Ben Chamberlain, Emma Cooke, Sarah Davey, Tara ffrench
Mullen, Philippe Le Moine, Neil McPherson, Cheryl Robson,
Michael Symons, Mountview Theatre School, The Riverside
Studios team, Julian Wadham, Romilly Weeks.
And to Marc Badrichani and Nicolas Tiffou.

The Little Black Book was originally programmed for
production at the Finborough Theatre, London.

JIMMY CHOO

LONDON ARTS

Association of
London Government

The Little Black Book
Jean-Claude Carrière
translated by Solvène Tiffou

British premiere at Riverside Studios, London, February 2003.

CHARACTERS	CAST
SUZANNE	Susannah Harker
JEAN-JACQUES	Paul McGann
Michel's voice	David Hollett
Director	Marianne Badrichani
Set and Costume Designer	Julie Marabelle
Light and Sound Designer	Steve Miller
Production Co-ordinator	Steve Harper
Assistant Director	Solvène Tiffou
Assistant Stage Manager	Helen Godfrey
Assistant Designer	Elizabeth Freeman
Make-up	Emily Thornton
Scenic Artist	Charlotte Gainey
Press Representative	Ben Chamberlain
Producers	Marianne Badrichani
	Solvène Tiffou

The setting:

A single set. A bachelor's studio flat in Paris, spacious and modern. Three doors: the entrance, the bathroom and the kitchen door. Large windows. A wardrobe with a mirror on the inside. A double bed, some chairs, a table, a combined bookshelf-bar. Something too meticulous, studied and actually cold about the decoration. Knick-knacks, stones, art books, cushions arranged all over the place. Most important and obvious to the viewer, a stuffed lizard about thirty centimetres long. A modern stylised television set and a sophisticated stereo. An entry phone by the door. A telephone. Several lamps. A large house plant.

PART ONE
SCENE 1

Nine o'clock in the morning. Jean-Jacques walks out of the bathroom, half-dressed. He quickly crosses the room to the kitchen, comes out, combs his hair in front of the wardrobe mirror. He then takes a black leather notebook, sits down and starts writing in it. He stands up, closes the notebook. Slightly distracted, he rapidly goes back to the bathroom. Sound of an electric razor.

A young woman pushes the door, which has been left ajar, and walks into the flat. She is plainly dressed, a travelling coat, or a raincoat. Her hands in her pockets. She looks around for a moment, then slowly walks up and down the room. She catches her reflection in the mirror, moves away, stands by the bed, stares at it.

Jean-Jacques walks out of the bathroom towards the wardrobe. He suddenly sees the woman in the mirror. He slowly turns towards her.

SUZANNE	Good morning.
JEAN-JACQUES	Good morning.
SUZANNE	I'm looking for Monsieur Ferrand.
JEAN-JACQUES afraid.	You don't have the right address, I'm
SUZANNE	You're not Monsieur Ferrand?
JEAN-JACQUES	No…
SUZANNE *(surprised)* Well.	

We hear the coffee maker whistling in the kitchen.

JEAN-JACQUES	My coffee, if you'd excuse me…
SUZANNE	By all means.

He goes into the kitchen. She follows him to the door.

SUZANNE   I thought it was here. I was told the fourth floor, on the left-hand side.

JEAN-JACQUES *(from the kitchen)* You are on the left side, but on the fifth floor. I'm sorry.

SUZANNE   I know, but there's no Monsieur Ferrand on the fourth floor, nor on the third.

JEAN-JACQUES *(from the kitchen)* I don't know any Monsieur Ferrand in the building.

SUZANNE   Or anywhere else?

JEAN-JACQUES *(after thinking a moment)* No, nowhere else.

SUZANNE   Your lift was out of order so I had to walk up. I would have asked the concierge but she wasn't there. I knew I should have waited. You wouldn't believe how awful your stairs are. I slipped. I nearly fell down. All I wanted was to see Monsieur Ferrand.

He comes back from the kitchen, holding a cup of coffee. He glances at her, startled, slightly worried.

JEAN-JACQUES   Are you sure you're in the right building? The right number?

SUZANNE   I've checked the entire street.

JEAN-JACQUES *(surprised)* Every single number?

SUZANNE   Some.

JEAN-JACQUES   And you're quite sure it's on the left. Fourth left?

SUZANNE   Who can be sure of anything now. *(looking at his cup)* Would you have a cup of coffee?

JEAN-JACQUES   You know what it's like, being single, I only made this one. Please, take it.

He offers her the cup, which she accepts as a matter of course.

SUZANNE   Thanks.
JEAN-JACQUES   Listen, I've got to hurry.
SUZANNE   Of course, do go ahead.

He exits into the bathroom to finish dressing. As soon as the door is closed, Suzanne puts her cup down and crosses to the front door.

SUZANNE   Your door was open so I walked in.
  I thought maybe I had the wrong address, or the wrong
  floor, that Monsieur Ferrand lived on the fifth floor. That's
  why I came up you see.

She exits and returns immediately carrying a large suitcase and a bundle of magazines. As she walks in, she adds.

SUZANNE   Since the door was open I just came
  in.
JEAN-JACQUES *(from the bathroom)* The door was open?
SUZANNE   Yes. How do you think I got here?

Jean-Jacques walks out of the bathroom to close the front door. As he turns back, he stops dead, seeing the suitcase and the magazines. He crosses to the wardrobe to get his shoes. He sits on the bed to put them on, looking increasingly surprised and uneasy.

JEAN-JACQUES   Have you checked the phone book?

The young woman picks up her cup and sits next to him, all friendly.

SUZANNE   You have no idea how many Ferrands there are in the phone book. They're all there, except the one I'm looking for. Naturally.

JEAN-JACQUES   Is he a relative?

SUZANNE   No, no…

JEAN-JACQUES   Why were you coming to see him?

SUZANNE *(with a vague gesture)* Oh…

JEAN-JACQUES   I'm sorry.

SUZANNE *(looking straight at him)* I hate the marble flooring in your staircase. It's really dangerous, you know. I slipped several times. I nearly fell. The trouble is no one uses stairs any longer. So they just put anything on them, like that marble. *(Getting up, she begins pacing up and down, looking about. Her questions come bubbling out.)* You only have this one room?

JEAN-JACQUES   Yes.

SUZANNE   Over there, is that the bathroom?

JEAN-JACQUES   Yes, it is.

SUZANNE   May I? I love to look at bathrooms! *(She pushes the door open and looks in.)* Oh, very nice. I'm very fond of that colour. You certainly have taste. *(quickly crossing the room)* And back there, is that the kitchen?

JEAN-JACQUES   It's tiny. I hardly ever use it.

He takes the empty cup to the kitchen. He is overly orderly.

SUZANNE   I see what you mean, it's more like a kitchenette. But it's well organised, and it's clean. *(She moves away from the door)* I can imagine it's very quiet in here.

JEAN-JACQUES *(returning)* Yes, it's very peaceful for a fifth floor. That's the main attraction of the place. The street is quite far down and when the window's closed, I can't hear a sound.

SUZANNE   Does the metro run under the
  building?
JEAN-JACQUES   No, it doesn't.

She is standing very close to the window, looking out. Jean-Jacques watches her, surprised. His replies are almost automatic.

SUZANNE   Do you get any sun in the afternoon?
JEAN-JACQUES   From four o'clock onwards.

She continues wandering around the flat while he fastens his tie. She then comes close to him, talking, and shows him her shoe. He is not interested.

SUZANNE   My feet are killing me… I just bought these and they're too tight. I knew it when I tried them on. But I liked the style, and they didn't have the next size up, so I took them anyway. And now my feet hurt.

She sits down. Jean-Jacques, almost ready, still watches her closely. She smiles at him.

JEAN-JACQUES   I'm sorry but I must leave. I have a meeting. I'm already late.
SUZANNE *(removing her other shoe)* Oh, I understand. These days everyone's late, especially me.
JEAN-JACQUES   If I didn't have to go, I'd be glad to…
SUZANNE *(surprised)* You work?
JEAN-JACQUES   Of course.
SUZANNE   What do you do?
JEAN-JACQUES *(putting on his jacket)* I'm a lawyer.
SUZANNE   Ah. Whereabouts?

JEAN-JACQUES   Rue de Londres. I have a partner
who's a friend. We have our own practice.

SUZANNE   And how are things?

JEAN-JACQUES *(perfuming his breast handkerchief)* Rather
quiet for the time being. It's the same everywhere. We're
setting up fewer companies than last year, plus real estate
isn't at its best. The general climate isn't…

SUZANNE   But overall, you're optimistic?

*He is ready. He says politely, while picking up a few
magazines she has spread around*:

JEAN-JACQUES   The concierge must be back by now.
You could ask her whether she knows this Monsieur
Ferrand, whether she's heard about him.

SUZANNE   Yes, why not.

JEAN-JACQUES   I'll come down with you, if that's all
right. Let me carry your suitcase.

SUZANNE   No, don't bother.

He picks up her suitcase and crosses to the door.

JEAN-JACQUES   It's a pleasure. I'll see you down.

SUZANNE   Would you mind if I stayed a little?

*Astonished, he is about to reply, when the phone rings. She
goes to answer it but he grabs the phone.*

JEAN-JACQUES *(on the phone)* Yes…? Oh it's you, hi
there. Is it that late? … *(He looks at his watch.)* I'll be there
in ten minutes… Tell them that I'm on my way… Michel!
Are you free this evening? … Joanna… She promised to

bring a friend... We'll see... All right... yes, yes, I'm coming.

While he is on the phone, the young woman takes a night gown and slippers out of her suitcase, a few magazines, and an alarm clock, without being seen by Jean-Jacques. She carefully puts the night gown on the bed. He turns towards her and stares at her in disbelief. Before he can speak.

SUZANNE   Now please don't be late on my account. I've been thinking seriously about Monsieur Ferrand. I'm not going to see him after all. It's better that way.

JEAN-JACQUES   Then why did you come in the first place?

SUZANNE   A personal matter. You don't mind if I stay?

JEAN-JACQUES   Here?

SUZANNE   Yes.

JEAN-JACQUES   I'd be happy to oblige you, but as you may have noticed, I'm leaving.

SUZANNE   That's all right.

JEAN-JACQUES   What do you mean – that's all right? *(She is slightly annoyed, as if he didn't understand her.)*

SUZANNE   I don't mind if you leave.

JEAN-JACQUES   You're telling me that I should leave you here alone?

SUZANNE *(putting her alarm clock on the bedside table)* Just for a while.

JEAN-JACQUES   Why would you want to stay here?

SUZANNE   You don't have to worry about your furniture. I won't touch anything, I promise. Really, you can trust me. *(walking back towards him)* Anyone can see you're very neat. I'm very fond of that. My school teacher used to say "When your desk is in order, your feelings are in order." *(She sits down.)* May I stay?

JEAN-JACQUES   How long?

SUZANNE   I'm so tired.

JEAN-JACQUES   Don't you know anyone around here?

SUZANNE   No. Not in this neighbourhood anyway. Thanks for asking.

JEAN-JACQUES   What about Paris? No one?

SUZANNE   I don't know Paris that well.

JEAN-JACQUES   Where are you from?

SUZANNE   Listen, when you've gone, I'll make your bed and I'll lie down for five minutes. I won't do anything else. I'll read a bit if I feel like it, then I'll leave. All right?

JEAN-JACQUES   Put yourself in my shoes for a minute, would you let a total stranger move into your home?

SUZANNE   I don't have a home.

JEAN-JACQUES   But if you did have a flat, would you? Would you accept it?

SUZANNE   Look, you don't have any money here, anything valuable?

JEAN-JACQUES   No.

SUZANNE   So what is there to worry about? Even if I were a thief.

JEAN-JACQUES   That's not the point. I'm sure you're honest, there's no doubt about that. It's just that I don't like the idea of leaving you alone in my flat, prying into my affairs.

SUZANNE   I don't have a habit of prying into other people's business. Prying around is not my thing. Not at all. And do I look like a slob? So stop worrying about your sweet home. I'll lie down on your bed for five minutes, and then I'll leave. *(slight pause)* What makes you think I'm an honest person?

JEAN-JACQUES   Go to a hotel.

SUZANNE *(suddenly in a low tense voice)* I have a living horror of hotels. I close my eyes whenever I walk past one. *(She takes the notebook and begins flipping through it.)* What kind of a book is this?

Jean-Jacques rushes and snatches it away, but not before she's understood.

JEAN-JACQUES   Don't touch that, it's nothing. Give it to me. You see, you're prying around already. I knew it.

SUZANNE   Is it a list?

JEAN-JACQUES   No.

SUZANNE   One does get the impression...

JEAN-JACQUES   Certainly not. *(He puts it away on the bookshelf, trying to hide it from her. But she sees him.)*

SUZANNE   I've got an idea.

JEAN-JACQUES   You do!

SUZANNE *(standing up)* If you're worried I'll steal something, lock me up. You'll just need to let me out tonight, when you come home.

JEAN-JACQUES   So now you're planning to stay all day?

SUZANNE   But you're forcing me to. You seem so terrified of the idea of my being here alone. As if the moment you turned your back, I'd burn your papers and cut up your clothes. When I can hardly move, when I've killed myself since dawn, up and down staircases with my suit-case! ... And you throw me out! As if your living-bath-kitchen room was a museum, the Holy of Holies! *(pause. Then in her usual voice.)* Who looks after this place?

JEAN-JACQUES *(conversationally)* There's a cleaning woman three mornings a week. She also takes care of the laundry.

SUZANNE *(moving towards him)* What about the cooking?

JEAN-JACQUES   Oh when I'm on my own in the evening, I do it. Easy things. Salmon, eggs, pasta with ham, cheese. But most of the time I go to restaurants.

SUZANNE   That must be boring in the end, and fattening besides.

JEAN-JACQUES   Yes and no. It's a matter of habit. You have to be careful and order just one thing. A steak, or fish maybe.

SUZANNE   I love fish! Fish and shellfish… especially sea urchins!

JEAN-JACQUES   Urchins, yes… and clams…

SUZANNE   Clams, winkles… *(pause)* So you have your own practice?

JEAN-JACQUES   Yes.

SUZANNE   Isn't that odd.

JEAN-JACQUES   Yes… What's odd about it?

SUZANNE   My father was a solicitor.

JEAN-JACQUES   He's dead?

SUZANNE   No, why?

JEAN-JACQUES   You said: my father was a solicitor.

SUZANNE   No, he's not dead. He's just no longer a solicitor.

The telephone rings. He picks it up. While he talks on the telephone, she takes the notebook and leafs through it.

JEAN-JACQUES *(to her)* Excuse me. *(on the phone)* Yes? … Well I'm doing my best… I know, I know… tell them I'm on my way… Can't you take care of it, yourself? Get the file from Lucy! Of course I'm alone… No, nobody! All right, all right, ten minutes…

He puts down the receiver and moves towards her. She quickly lets go of the notebook.

SUZANNE   You've got clients waiting?

JEAN-JACQUES   They're selling their business, quite a big deal. I was already late for the meeting before you even got here.

SUZANNE   Did you get up late?

JEAN-JACQUES   Yes.

SUZANNE   That's the life! Getting up late… When I can just lie around all morning, I'm fulfilled… One can't ask for more. *(abruptly pointing her finger at him)* You spent the night with someone, didn't you?

JEAN-JACQUES *(puzzled)* Who told you that?

SUZANNE   I think I passed her on the stairs. What was her name?

JEAN-JACQUES   Her name was… *(He thinks for a while)*… Florence.

SUZANNE   She must be the one who left the door open.

JEAN-JACQUES   Probably.

SUZANNE   She had dark hair, I remember…

JEAN-JACQUES   Yes, quite dark.

SUZANNE   Rather pretty.

JEAN-JACQUES   Yes, rather.

SUZANNE   Maybe a little… *(pause)* Is she in love?

JEAN-JACQUES   It's… embarrassing.

SUZANNE   Of course. I understand. *(She grasps the notebook and asks.)* What exactly is this book? *(Surprised for a moment, he takes back the book.)*

JEAN-JACQUES   It's nothing. Give it back.

SUZANNE   So it is what I thought, some kind of a list.

JEAN-JACQUES	Certainly not.
SUZANNE	I am no fool.
JEAN-JACQUES	I'm telling you that it is not a list.
SUZANNE	Then what? A diary? A datebook?

JEAN-JACQUES *(putting it away)* It's my little black book.

SUZANNE   What – age, weight, hair colour? Those kind of things?

JEAN-JACQUES	Maybe.
SUZANNE	What about pictures?
JEAN-JACQUES	If possible.
SUZANNE	Does it help?

JEAN-JACQUES   I can't remember anything. If I don't write it all down, I forget… as though it never happened.

SUZANNE	Really?
JEAN-JACQUES	Absolutely.
SUZANNE	What's the total so far?

JEAN-JACQUES *(perturbed)* Oh, I don't know.

SUZANNE   You know. You do know. Admit it.

JEAN-JACQUES *(embarrassed)* Doesn't interest me.

SUZANNE	A hundred? A hundred and fifty?
JEAN-JACQUES	Something like that.
SUZANNE	Exactly how many?

JEAN-JACQUES   As of this morning, of course I'd have to double check, it should be one hundred and thirty four.

SUZANNE   Is that a lot? I wouldn't know.

JEAN-JACQUES   It's… not bad. Statistically speaking, the average man knows twelve to fifteen women in his whole life.

SUZANNE	And the average woman?
JEAN-JACQUES	Less, I'd say.

SUZANNE   So a hundred and thirty four means you're above the average?

JEAN-JACQUES   Clearly. Listen, I'm not saying it's anything to brag about.

SUZANNE   Well… still!

JEAN-JACQUES   I'm sure there are notebooks a lot more significant than mine.

SUZANNE   Oh yes, of course, there must be! But you surprise me, more and more. You seem so… serious, at first sight.

JEAN-JACQUES   I am serious. No matter what I do, I do it seriously. *(pointing to the notebook)* There's the proof.

SUZANNE   May I see it?

JEAN-JACQUES   I said no.

SUZANNE   You mind?

JEAN-JACQUES   Well yes, I do. A bit.

SUZANNE   Why?

JEAN-JACQUES   I just do.

SUZANNE   I could be in it?

JEAN-JACQUES   No.

SUZANNE   You're sure?

JEAN-JACQUES   Pretty sure.

SUZANNE   I could have dyed my hair, changed my appearance. You promised me heaven a few years ago. Do you remember? And here I am. Only, you see there's a snag… you've forgotten me. You forget everything.

Jean-Jacques has been looking at her hesitating, searching.

JEAN-JACQUES   No, I don't know you. Definitely not.

SUZANNE   As far as I'm concerned, I don't find your hundred and thirty four all that impressive. Once I knew a prostitute. She was about forty, maybe forty-five, certainly no more. Well, she figured that in twenty, twenty-

five years in business she'd had around seventy-five
thousand men! So you see, you've still got some way to go.

JEAN-JACQUES   Where did you meet her?

SUZANNE   In the countryside.

JEAN-JACQUES   Could she have been somehow…
embellishing ?

SUZANNE   She was a very modest kind of person.
(slightly scornful) And by the way, without going as far as
her, I know lots of women who keep records, just like
yours. And believe me they do much better.

JEAN-JACQUES   For a woman, it's easier.

SUZANNE   Yes, it is easier, too easy I'd say. *(She
stands up.)* So can I see your book now?

JEAN-JACQUES   I told you, you're not in it.

SUZANNE   I'm curious.

JEAN-JACQUES   That's just too bad. *(She sits down,
slightly angry. He stands up and looks at his watch.)* I have
a feeling… that I ought to be doing something… that some
clients are waiting for me? Somewhere?

SUZANNE   You did mention something about a
practice.

JEAN-JACQUES *(suddenly)* Well, then. I'm off. *(showing
the notebook)* You won't touch it. Promise.

SUZANNE   Promise. *(While he is walking towards
the door, she adds.)* I won't be long. Thank you very much,
you're very kind.

JEAN-JACQUES   When the cleaning woman comes, just
ask her to do the usual.

SUZANNE   Don't worry. It will be immaculate.

*She lies down on her front, on the sofa with a bunch of
magazines. She leafs through two of them at a time without
looking at Jean-Jacques. He hangs around, almost gallant.*

JEAN-JACQUES   When you go, leave me an address where I can reach you… or a phone number.

SUZANNE   Certainly.

JEAN-JACQUES   Shall I ask the concierge about Monsieur Ferrand?

SUZANNE   Don't bother. I'll do it later.

Time passes. She turns and sees him standing by the bed.

SUZANNE   Do go away or Michel will lose his temper.

He walks towards the door, then comes back and asks.

JEAN-JACQUES   How do you know his name is Michel?

SUZANNE *(quick as a flash)* You said it on the phone.

Jean-Jacques turns and exits rapidly. Suzanne stands up briskly, and reaches for the little black book on the bookshelf. She returns to the bed leafing through it. She sits on the edge of the bed. She seems very interested, as if she were looking for something. The phone rings. She does not pick it up. Lights fade.

SCENE 2

Eight o'clock in the evening. Jean-Jacques' flat.
Suzanne is on her own. She is comfortably sitting amongst her
magazines. She is watching television, smoking. She is absent-
mindedly leafing through a magazine. She is listening to
music. The flat is rather messy: shoes, empty cigarette packs,
lots of magazines. The bed is untidy too; the night gown still
on it. After a while. Jean-Jacques enters in a rush. Seeing
Suzanne, he stops, startled.

JEAN-JACQUES   You, still here?

SUZANNE (*without moving*) Good evening.

JEAN-JACQUES   You've been here all day?

SUZANNE   Yes.

JEAN-JACQUES   You didn't even go out?

SUZANNE   Oh yes, I did some shopping. I bought
some cigarettes, the papers and some food. They fixed the
lift. The phone rang a few times but I didn't pick it up,
naturally.

He turns off the music.

JEAN-JACQUES   And Monsieur Ferrand?

SUZANNE   No news.

JEAN-JACQUES   You did try to find him?

No reply. She watches television without moving her face.

JEAN-JACQUES   Well? What are your plans?

SUZANNE   No plans for the time being.

Jean-Jacques walks around, appalled by the mess.

JEAN-JACQUES   Did the cleaning woman come?

SUZANNE   She did, this morning.

JEAN-JACQUES   Really? Doesn't look like it. *(He turns off the television.)*

SUZANNE   Sorry, I'll tidy up. Don't worry, it's nothing really, a matter of ten minutes.

JEAN-JACQUES   I'm in a hurry.

SUZANNE   Again?

He opens the wardrobe, takes out a dress and ask :

JEAN-JACQUES   What on earth is this?

SUZANNE   My dresses?

JEAN-JACQUES   You've hung them up, in this wardrobe?

SUZANNE   Yes. No use letting them get crumpled. I'll take them out if they're in the way. This second.

JEAN-JACQUES *(controlling himself with difficulty)* Where are my suits?

SUZANNE *(indicating the wardrobe)* There. *(He looks. She adds.)* In the back.

He bends and finds his clothes pushed in the back. He straightens up, empties his pockets to get changed.

JEAN-JACQUES   Now you listen to me.

SUZANNE   Yes.

JEAN-JACQUES   You are going to put everything back into your suitcase; you are going to pick up your magazines and you're going to be out of here in five minutes.

SUZANNE *(motionless)* All right.

JEAN-JACQUES   I'm sorry, but I'm late already.

Taking a suit from the wardrobe, he goes into the bathroom.
She stands up, takes the dress Jean-Jacques has just thrown on
the bed and hangs it back into the wardrobe, saying :

SUZANNE   Would you like an omelette before
you go? Or some rice with raisins and crab? I bought
masses of provisions.

JEAN-JACQUES *(from the bathroom.)* Take them with you.

SUZANNE   Oh no, I got them for you. I hardly
ever eat anything myself. You're sure? Aren't you hungry?

JEAN-JACQUES *(from the bathroom.)* I'm going out to
dinner.

SUZANNE   Ah…

She has an idea. She calmly puts on the night gown. She takes
off her trousers and throws them on the bed. Then she lies
down again. Meanwhile…

JEAN-JACQUES *(from the bathroom)* I've got friends
waiting downstairs. I was very busy today, since I started
so late. I'm just quickly getting changed and then I'm
rushing off. *(A pause, he shouts.)* They're waiting
downstairs!

SUZANNE   I am not deaf.

JEAN-JACQUES *(still from the bathroom)* I'm terribly sorry,
but your staying here is absolutely out of the question.

SUZANNE   I understand.

JEAN-JACQUES   Out of the question.

SUZANNE   Oh well, too bad! If you insist, I'll
leave, of course.

JEAN-JACQUES   I insist.

SUZANNE   In any case, I'm very grateful. I must
have slept two or three hours at least, I feel much better

now. The reason I stayed was to thank you. Your flat is
very soothing. I do like it after all. At first, I thought it was
a bit so-so, but actually it is very pleasant. Warm, quiet.
You really have to live in a place to appreciate it.

JEAN-JACQUES *(from the bathroom)* Are you ready?

*He has changed. He walks out to find her lying on the bed with
her eyes closed. He moves close to her meaning to talk. She
anticipates.*

SUZANNE	Do you handle property in your job?
JEAN-JACQUES	Yes, I do. *(He sits on the bed to put his shoes on, increasingly nervous.)*
SUZANNE	You haven't heard of a flat for rent by any chance?
JEAN-JACQUES	At this time of day?
SUZANNE	Where do you expect me to go?
JEAN-JACQUES	Don't you have any friends? Any relatives?
SUZANNE	Nobody.
JEAN-JACQUES	Then try the Salvation Army!

SUZANNE *(serious, nearly grave)* Don't mock me. It's not
funny. Try to understand. Help me, please. *(pause)* I'll tell
you exactly what I'm looking for – a modern studio flat,
doesn't have to be huge, just nicely decorated and
comfortable. *(gesturing around)* This kind of place. Only
on the top floor. As high as possible.

JEAN-JACQUES   I don't know of anything in particular.

SUZANNE *(indicating the newspapers)* Look, I bought all
those newspapers and read each and every advertisement.
For hours. You can't say I'm not trying. I looked very
carefully, every single column. I can assure you I found
nothing that suits me.

Jean-Jacques knots his tie, and puts on his jacket.

JEAN-JACQUES   That's no excuse for staying here.

SUZANNE   What would you do, if you were me?

JEAN-JACQUES   Take the first hotel.

SUZANNE (*sincerely affected*) I told you I cannot bear hotels. I'd rather sleep under a bridge or in a church hall.

JEAN-JACQUES   Sleep wherever you like, but not here. *(pause)* I'm not saying that to be cruel or unkind. I am a good man actually, gentle too. And rather amiable, I think.

SUZANNE   What makes you say so?

JEAN-JACQUES   People often come up to me in the street, asking for directions. At least once a day. Even tourists, beggars, charity ladies, shaking their cans. They come straight at me, every time. Doesn't that prove I'm rather amiable? Besides, I feel it inside. Whenever I can do somebody a favour, it makes me happy.

SUZANNE   It does ?

JEAN-JACQUES   It really does.

SUZANNE   I can make you happy.

JEAN-JACQUES   Oh?

SUZANNE   Let me stay here for a while. Do me a favour.

JEAN-JACQUES *(now ready to leave)* I am asking you, bluntly, to leave.

SUZANNE   It doesn't have to be this second, does it?

JEAN-JACQUES   Yes, it does. *(controlling himself)* Listen: this evening I'm going out with a friend... my partner.

SUZANNE   Michel.

JEAN-JACQUES   Michel. And two... young women.

SUZANNE   Indeed.

JEAN-JACQUES	We're going out to dinner.
SUZANNE	I know.

JEAN-JACQUES   Then we'll probably have a drink somewhere.

SUZANNE	Oh yes.
JEAN-JACQUES	Maybe we'll even dance.
SUZANNE	That's a good two or three hours.

JEAN-JACQUES   Approximately. Then – are you listening? Then it is quite possible – it is even extremely likely, that I'll come back here with one of these two young... ladies.

SUZANNE   Which one?

JEAN-JACQUES   That I don't know yet! One is called Joanna, she's French, she works for Unesco. I've seen her a couple of times, she's charming. However she's got a friend with her tonight whom I might like even better. We've just met. I find her quite attractive.

SUZANNE   I see.

JEAN-JACQUES   You just can't be here when we come back this evening.

SUZANNE   Why? I'd explain. I'd tell her how I just walked in looking for Monsieur Ferrand.

JEAN-JACQUES *(interrupting)* Listen! Listen.... euh… what's your name by the way ?

SUZANNE   What does it matter?

JEAN-JACQUES   Don't mess me around, I'm warning you.

SUZANNE   I'm not. I know what you're saying. You'll probably bring your friend home and if she finds me here, she'll leave, right?

JEAN-JACQUES   Right!

SUZANNE   I'd do the same if I were her. But she won't find me.

JEAN-JACQUES   She won't?

SUZANNE   Want to bet on it?

JEAN-JACQUES   No.

SUZANNE   I'll hide.

JEAN-JACQUES   There is nowhere to hide in this place.

SUZANNE   How much do you want to bet?

JEAN-JACQUES   Out of the question. I've given you five minutes to leave. I'm waiting.

SUZANNE   I could stay two or three hours anyway! Since you –

JEAN-JACQUES   Not even two or three minutes! Go on. Take your things and clear off!

He throws her suitcase on the bed. We hear a horn sounded impatiently on the street.

JEAN-JACQUES   You hear that horn? It's for me. I'm late again. Twice in one day. For someone who's always ferociously on time. That's my thanks for doing you a favour. It will teach me to leave my door open to the first –

SUZANNE   By the time you've had dinner and danced a little...

JEAN-JACQUES   Out!

He points to the door. Slowly, reluctantly, she collects a few magazines and takes them to her suitcase, picks up magazines.

SUZANNE   This girl you're bringing back here – not Joanna, the other one – what's her name?

He doesn't answer. She continues, slowly, to pack, takes a few dresses out of the wardrobe.

SUZANNE   She'll be number one hundred and
thirty-five, that's all.

JEAN-JACQUES   Now please, hurry up.

SUZANNE   I find this book-keeping utterly
depressing. On the one hand, there is something petty about
your list, but on the other hand it's endless. Somehow it's
ambitious – what a strange contradiction. It's almost like
using a stop watch to measure eternity.

*He is too surprised to reply. She takes the opportunity to go
on.*

SUZANNE   Is it very hard to seduce a woman?
JEAN-JACQUES   No… No, it's not hard…
SUZANNE   It's all in the technique, I suppose?
JEAN-JACQUES   Absolutely not.
SUZANNE   What then?
JEAN-JACQUES   It would take hours to explain.
SUZANNE   I'm in no hurry.

*Jean-Jacques is helping her, picking up magazines and putting
them into her bag. As he starts talking, he becomes engrossed
in his own words.*

JEAN-JACQUES   I haven't always been like this. When
I was seventeen or eighteen, I could barely look into a girl's
eyes. I'd steal a glance, but to turn and look directly, like
this… never… and yet that's what counts.

*She is sitting on the sofa, folding a few jumpers on her knees,
listening intensely, gazing at him.*

JEAN-JACQUES   Every time I sat next to a girl, I couldn't think of a word to say. I was tongue-tied. I then discovered that the most common phrases are the most effective, things like "I love the colour of your eyes" or "You're gorgeous." Anything, as long as you sound reassuring. In the end, no one's listening anyway. Why should they? They all know what's on your mind. The words just flow. The older you get the less you say. *(He sits.)* Then one day you wonder, how many? You add up, you find thirty, forty, with a few gaps. You're all proud. You'd never have expected so many. That's when you start your collection. You buy a notebook. You keep accounts. *(To himself)* All at once it becomes easy. Incredibly easy. I know that I've changed, that I dress better, that people trust me. And yet, that can't be the only reason. I just don't understand why it's so easy. *(pause)* Anyhow, believe it or not, whenever I look deep into a woman's eyes and she looks into mine, again and again... *(Their eyes meet. They look at each other in silence.)* What are you waiting for?

SUZANNE   I'm listening to you.

He stands, irritated with himself.

JEAN-JACQUES   Did I or did I not ask you to leave?
SUZANNE   You did.
JEAN-JACQUES *(harsh)* Well?
SUZANNE   I'm going. Of course, I'm going. I wouldn't spoil your evening for anything. But you might at least give me fifteen, twenty minutes to collect my things.
JEAN-JACQUES *(firmly)* No! My friends are waiting downstairs.... and I'm not leaving this place without you. I'm not even discussing it any longer. I've had it! *(He clears the remaining dresses out of the wardrobe.)* Move! Take these dresses, lock your suitcase, get dressed and come down with me. I'm giving you three minutes.

(He realises the consequences.) Oh no… don't come down with me. That's all I need, to be seen with you!

SUZANNE	Are they in the car with Michel?
JEAN-JACQUES	Yes.
SUZANNE	Right in front of the door?
JEAN-JACQUES	Right in front.
SUZANNE	Oh, how annoying!
JEAN-JACQUES	Indeed!
SUZANNE	There is a very simple solution.
JEAN-JACQUES	Which is?

SUZANNE   You go first and I'll follow in a minute.

JEAN-JACQUES   No, you go first. I'm the one who follows.

SUZANNE   As you wish. But it would be much easier to leave me here for a quarter of an hour so I could –

JEAN-JACQUES *(shouting)* All right, you asked for it. I'm going to throw you out. *(now completely mad)* I'm going to throw you out of that door myself.

He begins dragging her to the door, holding her wrist. She frees herself.

SUZANNE   Wait! Don't lose your temper. It makes you look deformed. You're ten years older. I'm leaving! I'm leaving! Let me just pack my suitcase and take it with me.

JEAN-JACQUES   Get on with it!

She is angry. She removes the magazines Jean-Jacques had put in the suitcase, scattering them back onto the floor. She then starts to pack, very meticulously, very slowly. Jean-Jacques watches, motionless.

JEAN-JACQUES　　That's right! Take your time!

SUZANNE　　I'm going as fast as I can.

JEAN-JACQUES　　You're a liar!

SUZANNE *(moving close to him)* Now what next? This morning you called me a thief, tonight you call me a liar. How reassuring do you think this is? I'm telling the truth. It's not my nature to hurry, that's all. I just can't help it. What I do, I do slowly. I've always been like that; that's how I was brought up. I'm slow… but at least I know what I'm doing.

Michel's horn sounds again, more and more insistent.

SUZANNE　　Your friends must be furious. You'd better go and let them know you won't be long.

JEAN-JACQUES　　So that you can hang your dresses back into the wardrobe and jump straight back to bed with your magazines.

SUZANNE　　With pleasure.

JEAN-JACQUES　　We're leaving!

SUZANNE　　Have you ever loved a woman?

JEAN-JACQUES *(quick)* One hundred and thirty-four.

SUZANNE　　That's not what I mean. Have you really...?

JEAN-JACQUES　　Shut up and hurry. Don't try to distract me. You can't trap me anymore!

SUZANNE　　Your friend, Michel – what's he like?

JEAN-JACQUES *(nonplussed)* What do you mean?

SUZANNE　　I mean, what's he like at his job? Clever? Conscientious?

JEAN-JACQUES　　He's all right.

SUZANNE　　Would he know of something for rent?

JEAN-JACQUES　　I don't know.

SUZANNE   You could ask him later on. And the
   ladies too, if you think of it.
JEAN-JACQUES   If I think of it.

Suzanne quickly sits on the edge of the bed.

SUZANNE   Give me a call to let me know. I'll be
   here by the phone. All right?
JEAN-JACQUES *(shouting)* You are not staying here! Go
   on! Get up! Right now!

*She starts to rummage through the wardrobe, drops a few
hangers and cries :*

SUZANNE   My blue dress, I've lost it. Have you
   seen my blue dress?
JEAN-JACQUES   Come on, it's in your suitcase! Are
   you ready now?
SUZANNE *(coming back towards him)* I have an idea. That
   woman you're bringing back here, Joanna, or the other
   one– maybe she could let me have her room for the night?
JEAN-JACQUES   No.
SUZANNE   Why not?
JEAN-JACQUES   It's out of the question.
SUZANNE   It's not true that you like to do favours.
   You have no sense of hospitality whatsoever. You are
   restless, bitter, selfish and unfeeling.
JEAN-JACQUES *(shouting)* Are you done?
SUZANNE *(shouting back)* But there has to be some place for
   me to go!

*Exasperated, he begins stuffing a pair of shoes into the
suitcase. He throws in her remaining dresses. She stops him.
Shouting at each other, they nearly come to blows.*

JEAN-JACQUES   Go wherever you like. I'd be only too
happy to help you get there.

They talk simultaneously.

SUZANNE   Don't touch my things. I have my own
special way of packing. Those shoes are too dirty. Are you
crazy? Leave that alone. Leave it alone. What's your
problem? You're hurting me!

JEAN-JACQUES   I'm warning you. I'm going to throw
this damn suitcase out of the window. If you're not out of
here in thirty seconds, I'll chuck everything out. That's all
you bloody deserve. And I'll also throw you down the
staircase, with your pretty little night gown on.

*He does as he says. He begins dragging the bag to the door.
She tries to hold him back. They struggle. The entry phone bell
rings. They freeze. Jean-Jacques presses the button. We hear
Michel's voice.*

MICHEL *(off)* Jean-Jacques!?
SUZANNE   Your name is Jean-Jacques?
JEAN-JACQUES *(releasing the button)* Shut up!
SUZANNE   Is that Michel?
JEAN-JACQUES   I said shut up!

The bell rings again. Jean-Jacques presses the button.

MICHEL. *(off)* What's going on? You're coming down or what? Hey, Jean-Jacques!

JEAN-JACQUES *(into entry phone)* I'm coming. I'll be straight there.

Leaving the entry phone, he shuts Suzanne's suitcase, leaving half the things hanging outside. Handing it to her, he opens the door.

JEAN-JACQUES   Take this and get out! Right now! This instant!

SUZANNE *(who is wearing a night gown)* Like this?! Look at me. How do you expect me to –

JEAN-JACQUES *(shouting)* Will you shut up!

The bell rings again. Jean-Jacques presses the button.

MICHEL *(off)* What's going on up there?

JEAN-JACQUES *(into entry phone)* Nothing.

SUZANNE   Half my things are hanging outside… you can't expect me to –!

JEAN-JACQUES *(releasing the button and yelling)* Shut up!

The bell rings. Jean-Jacques answers again.

MICHEL *(off)* Somebody up there with you?

JEAN-JACQUES   No!

SUZANNE   You really want me to leave this very instant?

JEAN-JACQUES *(screaming)* Shut the fuck up!

The bell rings again. Jean-Jacques out of control, presses the button:

MICHEL. *(off)* All right, that's enough, I'm coming up!

JEAN-JACQUES *(shouting)* No! I'm coming down. Didn't you hear me? I'm coming down! *(Absolutely furious, he turns towards Suzanne, threatening her.)* You're going to pay for that! I swear you'll pay for it. You'd better get out this second! And if I ever see your face round here again, I'll –

SUZANNE   All right, I'm leaving, I'm leaving!

The bell rings once more.

MICHEL *(off)* Are you coming?

JEAN-JACQUES *(calmly)* I'm coming.

He leaves. Suzanne picks up his hat. The moment he rushes back in, she hands it out to him. He takes it, puts it on and walks out.
Now alone, Suzanne, stands thinking. She takes a dress from the floor. At one point we think she will put it into her suitcase and leave. But no. She hangs it back into the wardrobe, calmly, as if she were at home.
Then she puts on some music. She gets the little black book she had hidden somewhere, lies back on the bed, and starts leafing through it.
Lights fade.

SCENE 3

*Morning. Suzanne, who has spent the night in Jean-Jacques'
flat, and Jean-Jacques' bed, is asleep. There are magazines
scattered on the bed and all around. Her suitcase is on the
floor, in a corner. The door of the wardrobe is ajar; Suzanne's
dresses are hanging inside. On the table, a pack of cigarettes,
nearly empty, a bottle of water, the alarm clock. A huge mess.
Jean-Jacques slowly walks in. He doesn't seem surprised to
find Suzanne asleep. For a moment, he looks at her. Then,
moving towards the kitchen, he stumbles against a piece of
furniture. The noise wakes Suzanne.*

SUZANNE	Hello.
JEAN-JACQUES	Hello.
SUZANNE here long?	Sorry, I was asleep. Have you been
JEAN-JACQUES	No, I just came in.
SUZANNE	What time is it?
JEAN-JACQUES you sleep well?	Half past eight, quarter to nine… Did

SUZANNE   Not too bad. I did have a hard time
falling asleep though. I had to take a light sleeping pill.
That's always how it is when I first sleep in a different bed.
(pause. She looks at him.) And you?

JEAN-JACQUES	I'm all right.
SUZANNE	You look all grey.

JEAN-JACQUES   At this time of day, I'm always
floating a little, I'm drifting in all directions.

SUZANNE   That's morning.

JEAN-JACQUES   Yes, that's morning. But when things
happen here, I feel more down to earth, more cheerful.

SUZANNE   I see what you mean.

At first, she seems a little apprehensive, as if she were expecting to be thrown out. The fact that Jean-Jacques shows no sign of violence, startles her. Suddenly, he starts talking to himself, as if he were recalling something. She sits up, resting against cushions.

JEAN-JACQUES   Women always sleep so well it gets on my nerves. One minute they're crying, right there, the next they're fast asleep. Just like that.

SUZANNE   I do apologise for last night.

JEAN-JACQUES   Oh, don't worry.

SUZANNE   You remember in the end you left so that your friend wouldn't come up. I thought: he's convinced I'm not moving from here, there's no way he'll bring back either of those women.

JEAN-JACQUES   Indeed.

SUZANNE   I was practically sure you weren't going to come back. So I stayed.

JEAN-JACQUES   I see.

SUZANNE   You're not angry, are you?

JEAN-JACQUES   No. No.

SUZANNE   You know yesterday, when you were throwing me out, I can assure you I had no idea where to go. I was lost, I panicked. You must have found me unbearable.

JEAN-JACQUES   Irritating maybe.

SUZANNE   I'm sorry. I'm so scared, all alone at night in the streets. But I won't do it again. I'll leave before twelve.

JEAN-JACQUES   There's no hurry.

SUZANNE   Thank you… You're not working today?

JEAN-JACQUES *(gloomy, lowering his head)* I work every day, apart from Saturday afternoons and Sundays. My first meeting is at half past nine. The Bugeot will. I'll be late today, like yesterday. This has never ever happened to me in my life. And yet I must have a wash, have a coffee and get changed.

SUZANNE   You seem to spend your life getting changed.

JEAN-JACQUES   How right you are.

She looks at him carefully.

SUZANNE   Have you already shaved?

JEAN-JACQUES   There was a razor over there.

SUZANNE   Where?

JEAN-JACQUES   Over there.

SUZANNE   Could I have some coffee?

JEAN-JACQUES (*without moving*) I'll get it.

SUZANNE   There's bread and marmalade in the kitchen.

JEAN-JACQUES   How about you making the coffee?

SUZANNE   I'm utterly incapable of such thing.

JEAN-JACQUES (*still not moving*) I suppose you've emptied your suitcase and hung all your clothes back into the wardrobe.

SUZANNE   Yes.

JEAN-JACQUES   Perfect.

SUZANNE   I couldn't possibly leave them all crammed in my suitcase, for the entire night.

JEAN-JACQUES   Of course not. (*pause*) I'll go and make some coffee.

He gets up slowly and walks into the kitchen, asking:

JEAN-JACQUES   What did you do last night?

Without raising her head, she raises her voice to answer.

SUZANNE   I had a light supper. I wasn't very
hungry. Then I watched television. There was a drama set
in Bohemia in the fourteenth century. Then I watched half
a football match between two Portuguese teams. Not bad.
I had a look at the paper. I tidied my things, brushed my
hair. I wasn't too keen on your little stuffed lizard so I
threw it down the rubbish chute.

*As she is talking, she stands up and replaces the notebook she
had kept under the cushions, on the bookshelf. Then she goes
back to bed.*

JEAN-JACQUES *(from the kitchen)* That's good.
SUZANNE   One more thing, I didn't know where
to put my suitcase. I did find the cupboard, but it was
packed with your own suitcases.
JEAN-JACQUES *(from the kitchen)* You should have taken
them out.
SUZANNE   I did think of it but I wasn't sure
where to put them!
JEAN-JACQUES   You should have thrown them out.
*(He returns from the kitchen carrying the breakfast tray as
if he were a waiter.)* There's your coffee. *(He lays the tray
on the bed. Suzanne starts to eat and drink, hungrily. Jean-
Jacques only takes a sip of the coffee.)*
SUZANNE   Oh thank you, nice and hot. I was
starving. That's Seville marmalade, I love it. *(She starts to
eat.)* How was your evening?

JEAN-JACQUES   Not bad. We had sushi for dinner, then we had a drink at Café Coste, then we ended up on the Rive Gauche as usual.

SUZANNE   Did your friends know of anything for rent?

JEAN-JACQUES   I forgot to ask.

SUZANNE   There you are! How do you expect me to leave if you don't do anything to help. *(She takes a sip of coffee and adds.)* Your coffee's not too bad for a bachelor.

JEAN-JACQUES   I'll make some more if you want.

SUZANNE   Thank you.

Jean-Jacques puts down his cup, stands up without a word to take his notebook from the bookshelf. He opens it, takes a pen, and writes a few words. He is quite gloomy. Still eating in bed, she follows him with her eyes.

SUZANNE   Don't you ever cheat?

JEAN-JACQUES   What do you mean?

SUZANNE   The things you write in your book, they're always rigorously accurate?

JEAN-JACQUES   Rigorously. *(showing the book)* Did you look at it?

SUZANNE   I couldn't sleep, I was a bit bored… Anyway, as you noticed, I put it back in the right place. And I only read the beginning, after that I just skimmed through it. What a drag. It's always the same.

JEAN-JACQUES   It's not something you're meant to read.

SUZANNE   In the photographs, they're practically always smiling… By the way, yesterday, you didn't tell me – was it Joanna?

JEAN-JACQUES   No, the other one.

SUZANNE	I thought so. Try to describe her.
JEAN-JACQUES	That's not easy.
SUZANNE	Her size? Her weight?
JEAN-JACQUES	I didn't interrogate her. She had dark hair. Eyes… rather light. Tiny.
SUZANNE	What was her name?
JEAN-JACQUES	Catherine. But we called her Doudou.
SUZANNE	And you never met her before?
JEAN-JACQUES	No.
SUZANNE	Can I have your toast?
JEAN-JACQUES	It's for you.

SUZANNE *(taking the toast)* In your book, there's a woman you've entered twice, three years apart. Exactly the same one. A certain Gabrielle. Did you actually realise the second time?

JEAN-JACQUES Not while I was at it.

SUZANNE What about her? Did she recognise you?

JEAN-JACQUES I don't think so.

SUZANNE You seduced her twice. You asked her the same questions twice and she never noticed anything? Poor Gabrielle.

JEAN-JACQUES At least she didn't mention anything. No allusion. No embarrassment.

SUZANNE In your total, do you count her as one or two?

JEAN-JACQUES Two.

SUZANNE I know it's your own business, but I'd never even consider such a thing. Oh no, really. A cold succession of entries in a notebook. With all the moves, the tricks, the wasted time, the shame. When I remember, I remember my own feelings.

He briskly stands up as if she were annoying him, comes close to the bed and asks dryly.

JEAN-JACQUES   What's your name?

SUZANNE *(suddenly worried)* Oh please.

JEAN-JACQUES   Give me your name.

SUZANNE   I don't want to.

JEAN-JACQUES   I can't go on talking to you if I don't know your name.

SUZANNE   Well then, stop talking to me!

JEAN-JACQUES *(loudly)* For me it's the most important thing. I need to be talking to a person, a name. It's the first thing I ever ask. I've met three women who refused to tell me their names, for one reason or another. *(He nearly screams.)* I swear, I didn't count them. They're not in here!

SUZANNE   All the more reason to keep quiet.

JEAN-JACQUES *(stepping aside)* Sorry, I didn't make myself clear. Don't judge me by the way I act this early in the day.

SUZANNE   I wouldn't dream of judging you.

JEAN-JACQUES *(suddenly)* I thought about you all night long.

Silence. He takes the tray to the kitchen. Then he puts things straight to hide his emotions. She watches him in a new way, interested, slightly fearful.

JEAN-JACQUES   I got up earlier than usual to come back here. Usually, I go straight to the office. I drove like mad. I didn't even look for a parking place. I left my car on the pelican crossing, can you imagine, on the crossing! … I wanted to know what had become of you. Oh, don't get me wrong, if you hadn't been there, I couldn't have cared less. Well, I mean, I wouldn't have been unhappy. Certainly not.

Not even disturbed. At least no more than usual. But at least I would've known where I stood. Like now.

SUZANNE   My name is Suzanne.

He stops talking and looks at her with an air of strong displeasure.

JEAN-JACQUES   But I don't like the name!

SUZANNE   That doesn't surprise me.

JEAN-JACQUES   Definitely, absolutely not!

SUZANNE   I knew it.

JEAN-JACQUES   Why do you have to be called Suzanne?

SUZANNE   It's only a name, I'm sorry. I shouldn't have told you. I knew you'd hate it. Everybody hates it. Who would think of calling their daughter Suzanne nowadays? Who? I wonder!

JEAN-JACQUES   Sometimes parents forget to think.

SUZANNE *(irritated)* It's not my fault, all right! My name's Suzanne and I can't help it!

JEAN-JACQUES   Forget what I just said. It doesn't matter. Hang on a minute, there is one thing I'd like to know… Just a second. *(He stands up and gets the notebook on the coffee table, opening it on the last page. The phone rings. He answers still holding the book.)* Yes? … Hello… You're sure? My watch must have stopped, sorry… Yes, you're right, tell Madame Bugeot that I'm on my way… yes, it went all right… Rue des Bons Enfants... This evening, I can't say yet, I don't know…

Suzanne starts talking from the bed. He puts his hand on the receiver so that Michel can't hear her.

SUZANNE   Please don't change your plans on my
account!

JEAN-JACQUES *(to Suzanne)* Shut up. *(on the phone)* We'll
talk later OK? Yes I'm coming… My car's parked right in
front of the house, bye.

He hangs down and looks at the notebook again. A pause.

SUZANNE   You're checking the notebook?
JEAN-JACQUES   No Suzanne…
SUZANNE   I know, I've already checked…

He raises his head and gazes into the air.

SUZANNE   I don't like what you're thinking.
JEAN-JACQUES   Sorry. *(He briskly closes the notebook
and moves away.)*
SUZANNE   God knows how indulgent I am! You
must have noticed, I let you get away with anything.
JEAN-JACQUES   You're joking?
SUZANNE   No.
JEAN-JACQUES   I'm the one who's indulgent! I'm the
one who has to put up with you! I'm the one who's patient
and generous. *(She says no with her hand.)* Aren't I?
SUZANNE   It's the other way round. Think about
it: first I keep you company, you said so yourself, and
nowadays that's priceless. I'm no more foolish or hideous
than the next girl. And I dedicate all my time to you. I'm
here, at your disposal. I chat, I distract you, I make you
late: isn't that wonderful? And as soon as the conversation
peters out, I make you talk about yourself. That's your
favourite topic, you lap it up, you just love it. *(pause)* You
don't appreciate what I'm worth.

JEAN-JACQUES Why are you harassing me? What do you want from me? Who are you?

SUZANNE Too many questions at once. I refuse to answer.

JEAN-JACQUES If I really want to find out, I will.

SUZANNE You won't find out anything.

JEAN-JACQUES I've got friends who work in the police force.

SUZANNE I don't.

A pause. He moves away.

JEAN-JACQUES *(weary)* I have to go now.

SUZANNE Stay.

JEAN-JACQUES It won't get any better if I stay. I'm leaving.

SUZANNE It's a shame. There's no reason to hurry.

JEAN-JACQUES *(after a moment)* Anything you need?

SUZANNE Don't trouble yourself. And if you have another of your rendezvous tonight, do go. I can very well stay by myself. It doesn't bother me at all.

JEAN-JACQUES You're lucky… Good bye.

He stands by the bed, where she is lying once more, buried in cushions. Her eyes are closed. He looks at her.

SUZANNE There is one thing, if you think of it!

JEAN-JACQUES Yes?

SUZANNE The newspapers. So that I can go on looking for a flat.

JEAN-JACQUES All right.

He walks to the door in no hurry. He leaves reluctantly.

SUZANNE *(gently mocking him)* Do work carefully. Be
   precise. Be polite but firm… You didn't get changed?

JEAN-JACQUES   No time for that.

SUZANNE   Is the cleaning woman coming?

JEAN-JACQUES   Not today, tomorrow… have a nice
   day.

SUZANNE   You too… I'll tidy up, don't worry.

Before leaving, he turns around one last time.

JEAN-JACQUES   Aren't you going to get up?

SUZANNE   When you've left.

*He slowly takes his attaché case, his hat and walks out without
turning round again.*
Lights fade.

SCENE 4

*Late at night. The furniture has been moved around. On the
table, the leftovers of a luxurious dinner, with a bottle of
champagne. Low lights, a large bouquet of flowers: an air of
conventionality. Jean-Jacques is standing by the kitchen door.
From the kitchen we hear the tinkling of glasses and
Suzanne's voice. She comes out wearing an elegant evening
outfit. They sit opposite each other.*

SUZANNE   My father was a solicitor in the
provinces. A lawyer, just like you. As I said, his name is
Hotteneuve. My mother died eleven years ago... One
summer night at a party, I meet a young Parisian on
holiday, called Philippe Ferrand. After the dance, we go for
a stroll down to the river. We lie down for a few minutes
beneath poplars; I become pregnant. *(pause)* I came to
Paris to look for Philippe. He'd run away, the next day.
(long pause)

JEAN-JACQUES   Go on.

SUZANNE   It doesn't go on, that's all there is.

JEAN-JACQUES   So he's the Philippe Ferrand you were
looking for yesterday morning?

SUZANNE   No. Not yesterday. That was last year.

JEAN-JACQUES   Here? At this address?

SUZANNE   No, not at all.

JEAN-JACQUES   Why did your father sell his practice?

SUZANNE   What do you think, for a woman.

JEAN-JACQUES   What about the child?

SUZANNE   Which one?

JEAN-JACQUES   The one with Philippe Ferrand, last
year.

SUZANNE   He was never born.

Silence. Jean-Jacques picks up a book from the floor and opens it.

SUZANNE *(looking at him)* You should have dined out with Michel. This book is boring you.

JEAN-JACQUES   It's not that it's boring me, it's just that I'm not used to reading, so I find it tiresome.

SUZANNE   I can read just about anything. Anything that's printed. With the same kind of interest. *(She picks up a newspaper.)* I've ticked two advertisements. A sunny one bedroom on the fourth floor, in the ninth arrondissement, Rue des Martyrs. And a studio flat in Montparnasse, on the eighth floor, for 31,430 francs per month. I'll go and see them tomorrow morning.

JEAN-JACQUES   5 000 euros. Isn't it very expensive?

SUZANNE   No, that's the going rate. You should know.

JEAN-JACQUES   Do you have money?

SUZANNE   A little.

JEAN-JACQUES   Where did you get it?

SUZANNE   When my father went bankrupt, my mother sold all her belongings. We split what was left with my brother.

JEAN-JACQUES   I thought your mother was dead.

SUZANNE   Yes, after that, she died of a broken heart.

JEAN-JACQUES   Tell me honestly, do you work for a living?

SUZANNE   My life is totally inactive. I can't do anything, I can't sew a button, prick a slice of mutton, plant a tulip, drive a car. Nothing. And I refuse to learn.

JEAN-JACQUES   You're against women working?

SUZANNE   Yes. And men too.

JEAN-JACQUES   Where was your father's practice?

SUZANNE *(lying down)* I'm very good at resting. It's not as easy as people think. My dream is a house where everything is automatic. All you'd need to do is press buttons. I'd just have to think of a glass of water, someone would bring it to me. Magazines would turn their pages by themselves. Clothes would come and dress me on their own. My body would disappear step by step. *(pause)* And yet tomorrow morning, by some terrible fate, I will have to get dressed, take the lift down, find a taxi, ring doors, visit flats, speak to people. Just the kind of day I hate.

JEAN-JACQUES   Don't think about tomorrow.

SUZANNE   I can't think of anything else.

JEAN-JACQUES   I wish my flat was bigger. It was really only made for one.

SUZANNE   Yes, I could really make do with it. Even with you. I wouldn't be in your way. I hardly move. But I understand how you can't keep me here. I really understand. It's only natural. What time do you usually go to bed?

JEAN-JACQUES   There's no rule.

SUZANNE   I'm going to make a confession. I'd made up my mind to leave this morning. Before you came back. I felt I had to. I'd even started to pack. But you caught me by surprise. When I saw you coming home with flowers, champagne and seafood, I thought staying a bit longer was the right thing to do. And now it's so late. It must be at least two in the morning?

JEAN-JACQUES   I've lost track.

SUZANNE   May I request your official permission to stay for the night.

JEAN-JACQUES   I didn't intend to throw you out.

SUZANNE   You're not the kind of person to do that.

JEAN-JACQUES   If my being here bothers you, I can spend the rest of the night at a friend's house. Or at a hotel.

SUZANNE   Of course I don't mind your being here. If I did, I'd have left long ago. I know I'm lazy but still, not to that extent… *(leaning towards him)* You hardly ever look me straight in the eyes. I have a feeling you don't know your own mind.

JEAN-JACQUES   At this very second, I have only one desire – to stay exactly in the same position. Sitting. Motionless. Silent.

Smiling, she pours him a glass of champagne.

SUZANNE   You're right. The night is shorter than the day, and not quite as dreadful. Let us face it together. Cheers!

JEAN-JACQUES   Cheers!

They make a toast, and hardly drink anything. She puts her glass on the floor and lies down.

JEAN-JACQUES   Are you not feeling sleepy?

SUZANNE   I'm constantly sleepy, only not at night.

JEAN-JACQUES   Tell me more about yourself

SUZANNE   But why do you insist on knowing my name, where I'm from, what my parents do, whether I have a job? What does it matter? Why can't you be satisfied with me? *(pause, she smiles.)* Forget about my appearance and content yourself with my essence. That's how people believe in God.

JEAN-JACQUES   What's the matter with you?

SUZANNE   Vague memories. *(A silence. They look at one another. She sighs.)* I give up. So what should I talk about? My parents?

JEAN-JACQUES   Your lovers.

SUZANNE   Of course. But I'm warning you. We don't necessarily have the same problems, you and I. I have forgotten a lot, even more than you.

JEAN-JACQUES   You don't have to talk…

SUZANNE   That's not what I said.

JEAN-JACQUES   I'm all ears, be precise. *(pause)* So?

SUZANNE   I'm pondering…

JEAN-JACQUES   Or making it up?

SUZANNE   …whatever I say is true. From the moment ideas become words...

JEAN-JACQUES   And what you don't say?

SUZANNE   …doesn't exist.

JEAN-JACQUES   Your lovers.

SUZANNE   Be patient; I'm getting there. *(She takes a sip of champagne.)* It all depends on when I'm asked and who does the asking. Sometimes it seems like I've roamed in hundreds of beds like you. On carpets too, on sand, on grass, in cars, behind bathroom doors. I've been around, I've got thirty years of vice behind me. My skin is worn out and coarse like an old piece of wood. And it's true, some days it's true. *(pause)* At other times, I'm an ordinary woman. I had four or five lovers my age before I got married and three or four afterwards. Nothing much worth mentioning. I don't really like love-making. I'm waiting for my prince charming and slowly withering. *(She straightens up.)* Then, there are times, but less frequent, when I'm a virgin. Immaculate. Very proud, even arrogant. Rather happy. *(pause)* See, tonight for instance, that's how I feel. It's actually more than a feeling, it's a fact. Tonight, I am a virgin. I swear I am. *(She bends over and very gently* *strokes Jean-Jacques' hand. He doesn't move.)* You are the first man I ever touched.

JEAN-JACQUES   How I wish I could talk like you.

SUZANNE   You do believe me?

JEAN-JACQUES   Oh yes, I believe you. Always. Whether you say black, whether you say white, I only want to believe in you. I am utterly incapable of contradicting you. *(pause)* You frighten me.

SUZANNE   Yes, I've just realised that. I wonder why.

JEAN-JACQUES   I feel shy.

SUZANNE   A man like you?

JEAN-JACQUES   I can't make up my mind whether to walk to you and take you in my arms…

SUZANNE   Maybe that's what I'm waiting for.

JEAN-JACQUES   But what if I'm wrong, imagine the shame.

SUZANNE   You have gone back in time.

JEAN-JACQUES   Yes.

SUZANNE   A woman is sitting next to you, in your own flat, and yet, you remain silent. She just needs a word, but which one? What about those reassuring phrases? Those useful words?

JEAN-JACQUES   Lost.

SUZANNE   Try.

JEAN-JACQUES   No.

SUZANNE   Am I too accessible?

JEAN-JACQUES   On the contrary.

SUZANNE   I don't understand.

JEAN-JACQUES   There's one thing you must know, deep down I'm not very happy with myself.

SUZANNE   No.

JEAN-JACQUES   I've no courage.

SUZANNE   It doesn't take much.

JEAN-JACQUES   That's what you think.

SUZANNE   Isn't your well-organised life supposed to bring you peace? What does courage have to do with it?

JEAN-JACQUES   I wasn't talking about the others. I was talking about you. If I had to describe you, I couldn't do it. I can't even remember the colour of your eyes. *(He looks at her for an instant.)* I can't see you. *(He looks away.)* I wish I didn't know your name.

SUZANNE   Try to forget it.

JEAN-JACQUES   I won't ask you any more questions. I don't want to know anything about you, not your father's name, not your lovers'. You arrived yesterday morning and you're called Suzanne. That's all I know. That's how it should be.

SUZANNE   All right.

JEAN-JACQUES   I see your suitcase packed and unpacked, your dresses coming and going. You mentioned a Monsieur Ferrand. I don't know whether you're really looking for something in the papers. Last night I wanted to throw you out, tonight I won't see you leave. *(pause)* We could take a larger flat.

SUZANNE   What's wrong with this one?

JEAN-JACQUES   It's too small.

SUZANNE   I don't take up much room.

JEAN-JACQUES *(louder)* You're the one who said it was too small.

SUZANNE   I said such a thing? Did I really?

JEAN-JACQUES   I can still hear you say it. *(Suddenly he looks suspiciously at Suzanne.)* What is it with you and this flat? Did you live here before?

SUZANNE   No.

JEAN-JACQUES   That's what it is. You lived here with
another man. He was the one you hoped to find when you
came here yesterday!

SUZANNE   Calm down.

JEAN-JACQUES   Who is this 'Monsieur Ferrand' on the
fourth floor left? I have a feeling I knew someone with that
name. He lived here before me? He's the last owner?

SUZANNE   Please shut up! Don't start again.

JEAN-JACQUES   I'm sorry.

SUZANNE   Keep calm, otherwise I'll have to go.

JEAN-JACQUES *(standing up)* No, no. You've got nothing
to fear any longer. I promise. I'll never ask anything again.
I'm trembling. I want to quarrel with you. Any excuse
would do. I'd like to swear at you. But I can't. I'm fighting
the desire to disappear from your sight and run as fast as I
can.

SUZANNE   That's something I'd like to see.

JEAN-JACQUES   And I'd like to take a shower, to eat,
to cut paper into pieces, to listen to the news. *(shouting)* To
do something. You understand. To distract myself!

SUZANNE   Please feel at home.

JEAN-JACQUES   Help me. Stop staring at me like that.
Take the first step if you can.

SUZANNE   It's not really my thing…

JEAN-JACQUES   But what was I thinking… *(He stands)*
Let's do the usual set up to spur me on. First the music… It
works every time. Listen. *(He puts the same CD on again,
gentle modern music.)* Then I spray a musky scent all over
the room. *(He does so.)* For musk is known to prevent the
heart from falling asleep. *(He goes towards the switches.)*
Then I turn down all the lights. Nearly all… It never fails.
(He moves hesitantly towards her.) I feel much better
already… Come…

She stands and moves towards him. They stand facing each other, they look at each other for a while. All of a sudden, he moves away, stops the music, sits back on the sofa and says:

JEAN-JACQUES I love you.

She moves slightly towards him, puts her knee on a stool which stands between them and says smiling:

SUZANNE I thought so.

As she puts her arms around Jean-Jacques' neck, blackout.

PART TWO
SCENE 5

*It's about two o'clock in the afternoon. The flowers and the
empty bottle are still there. Day after the party sort of mess.
Nobody in the flat. Jean-Jacques rushes in with a smile.*

JEAN-JACQUES   Hello! *(No answer. He crosses the
room, takes a look into the kitchen, into the bathroom.)*
Suzanne!

*Suzanne enters through the front door behind him, without him
seeing her. He goes towards the wardrobe thinking she may be
locked in it. He throws open the doors and shrieks. He closes
the doors disappointed. He turns round and sees Suzanne.*

SUZANNE *(smiling)* I saw you coming in downstairs. Didn't
you hear me call?

JEAN-JACQUES   No.

SUZANNE   You were running like a lunatic.

JEAN-JACQUES   I generally don't come home at this
time of day, I haven't the time. Today I had five minutes
after lunch, so I thought I'd say hello.

SUZANNE   That's sweet of you.

JEAN-JACQUES   Have you been out long?

SUZANNE   Yes, I left right after you.

JEAN-JACQUES   Where have you been?

SUZANNE   I think I've found a flat.

JEAN-JACQUES   Where?

SUZANNE   In a modern building, Rue de Paradis.
It's a large studio with a terrace, on the top floor. Slightly
expensive, but superb. There's sun all day long. And it's
vacant.

JEAN-JACQUES	So it's exactly what you're looking
for?	
SUZANNE	Exactly.

Rather ill at ease, he starts to empty the ash trays, to reorganise the furniture. He takes the empty bottle into the kitchen and comes back.

JEAN-JACQUES	And you're going to – move there?
SUZANNE	Yes, definitely. I absolutely loved it.
JEAN-JACQUES	Soon?
SUZANNE	As soon as possible.
JEAN-JACQUES	So it's all done? All settled?
SUZANNE	Nearly. I still need to sign the lease.
Just formalities.	

Pause. Jean-Jacques goes back to the kitchen.

JEAN-JACQUES	Would you like some lunch?
SUZANNE	Thanks. I've had lunch already. The
man from the agency invited me. Charming young man.	
There's a very nice wine bar just opposite my new home.	

As she is talking, she opens her suitcase, which is still in the same place, and starts rummaging in it. It seems very messy. Finally, she finds some crumpled bits of paper.

SUZANNE	We've just finished our lunch. He
drove me back here. He's waiting for me downstairs.	
JEAN-JACQUES	Now?
SUZANNE	Yes.
JEAN-JACQUES	What for?

SUZANNE *(showing her papers)* I just came by to get my
  papers for the signing. And my cheque book. Oops, I'd
  better not forget that. *(She takes her cheque book.)* I must
  run. I didn't expect to find you here. If I'd known of
  course, I'd have taken time to –

JEAN-JACQUES   Is it really big this studio?

SUZANNE   Oh yes!

JEAN-JACQUES   Bigger than here?

SUZANNE   Huge. The kitchen for instance, is a
  real kitchen, completely equipped. And there's carpet all
  over the place, and a long sunken bath tub. As for the
  terrace, it's enchanting. It's got lovely sweet peas and
  marigolds. You can even see the Eiffel Tower in the
  distance. You'll come won't you. I'll be so happy.

JEAN-JACQUES   When are you leaving?

SUZANNE   I don't know, maybe this evening.

JEAN-JACQUES   So soon...?

SUZANNE   I have so little with me. Nothing but
  my suitcase. Tomorrow at the latest. *(She walks towards
  the door.)* You have to see my terrace. It's amazing!

JEAN-JACQUES   How much is it a month?

SUZANNE   Not cheap. I don't have the exact
  figure though. It's per term.

JEAN-JACQUES   Are the charges included?

SUZANNE   I suppose so.

JEAN-JACQUES   Don't you like it here?

SUZANNE   Yes, of course I do, you know that.
  (Jean-Jacques is silent. She turns towards him.) If I didn't
  like your flat, I wouldn't have stayed five minutes. It's just
  that… To start with, you were right, it's really too cramped
  for two people, even if they're not the moving around kind.
  And then, well, a fifth floor is slightly too low, you only
  get sun in the afternoon. *(She looks around, wondering.)*
  Well, you see… it is your flat after all.

JEAN-JACQUES   Of course.

SUZANNE   You certainly made sure I was aware of that.

JEAN-JACQUES   That's true.

SUZANNE   I've imposed myself on you long enough. Do you realise –? Three days, that's a long time. I'm going to free you from my presence. *(She turns round and starts towards the door.)*

JEAN-JACQUES   Hang on, just hang on a moment. Tell me something… You do have a minute to spare, don't you?

SUZANNE   There is this little man waiting for me downstairs.

JEAN-JACQUES   Is he in a hurry?

SUZANNE   What do you mean?

JEAN-JACQUES *(slightly embarrassed)* Listen, if you come to think of it, I don't own that much. There aren't that many things that I really care about. My washing things, my clothes, a couple of papers. Everything would fit into two suitcases. Or one suitcase and a bag. All the rest, the knick-knacks, the furniture, I can easily get rid of it, or just leave it here.

SUZANNE   Where would you go?

JEAN-JACQUES   To your flat. *(A short silence.)* Of course I'd take care of the bills. We can sell this flat, I own it. We'll invest the money. Or we'll get a house in the countryside, in the South… *(She looks at him gravely. He looks away.)* There's another option. We don't sell the flat, but we rent it furnished. I'd have to look into that. *(moving close to her)* I haven't seen your studio yet, but I love it already.

SUZANNE   You mean you want to come to my flat?

JEAN-JACQUES   Yes, that's what I mean.

SUZANNE   For a long time?

JEAN-JACQUES　　Well, yes for a long time…

SUZANNE　　You think that's the least I can do, don't you?

JEAN-JACQUES　　No, no, of course not! What are you thinking? You don't owe me anything. *(pause)* Forget the whole idea. I never mentioned it.

SUZANNE　　Please don't start telling me I'm ungrateful. I haven't forgotten anything you did for me. The flowers, the champagne – I'm extremely grateful. But what's that got to do with living in my flat? If you want to pay me a visit now and then, of course. As often as you like. You'll always be welcome Jean-Jacques. I'll even give you a key. But to live in my flat! That's another story! I've been wanting to live on my own for such a long time, to be totally independent. It must be so nice, to be alone, at night, once your friends have left, in a place you've chosen, arranged. A room of one's own. *(She dreams.)* Why get in each other's way? All cramped? You do understand what I mean?

JEAN-JACQUES　　It's extremely clear.

SUZANNE　　I don't know how to explain. It's so awkward.

JEAN-JACQUES *(weary)* You don't need to, I understand perfectly well.

SUZANNE　　I'll invite you to dinner. If you want to help me move in, that's fine too. There's some painting to be done. Come this evening! Yes? You'll be the first one.

JEAN-JACQUES　　Maybe. I don't know what I'm doing tonight.

SUZANNE　　But to move in permanently… does seem over the top.

JEAN-JACQUES　　Once again, I apologise.

SUZANNE　　Why not get married under such circumstances?

A pause.

JEAN-JACQUES *(as if it were obvious)* We could get
   married. *(She looks at him, surprised.)* You don't want to?
SUZANNE   No. *(pause)* I'm not cut out for
   marriage. I'm much too passive. It would be a nightmare.
   You're down to earth Jean-Jacques. You never lose track of
   your business, your investments. We would be unhappy as
   a couple, I never think about anything you see, never ever.
   (Sound of a horn) Do you hear him? What nerve? He's
   hooting for me!

Jean-Jacques stands in front of the closed entrance door.

JEAN-JACQUES   Will he be living with you?
SUZANNE   Are you out of your mind? He's the
   manager of the agency!
JEAN-JACQUES   I'm not sure about any of this.
SUZANNE   Let me out.
JEAN-JACQUES   No.

Suzanne tries to go out.

JEAN-JACQUES *(seizing her by the arm)* Don't leave!
SUZANNE   What's the matter with you?
JEAN-JACQUES *(laughing)* I forbid you to leave! Do you
   hear me! I won't let you leave this place!

*The phone rings. Jean-Jacques remains immobile, looking at
the phone, worried.*

JEAN-JACQUES   Don't… Wait a minute… Come…
   (He pulls her towards him, dragging her towards the

phone. He answers.) Yes? *(He talks in a low and desperate voice.)* Yes, I know… I'm not coming this afternoon… The Bugeot will, I don't give a shit… The old lady, same thing. All right, put her on. *(shouting)* Madame Bugeot. Good afternoon Madame… Yes. There's something I want to tell you... first of all, I don't give a damn about your will, and secondly you're a stupid old cow so please bugger off… That's all… I'm fine, thank you… *(shouting)* Pass me back to Michel… *(to Suzanne)* She's passing me back to him. *(on the phone)* Hello... Yes, I told her to go and… precisely … yes… by the way, same for you. No, I won't be coming in tomorrow. I can't be fucked. *(He hangs up wearily and doesn't move. He lets go of Suzanne's hand. A silence.)*

SUZANNE Jean-Jacques? *(No answer)* I've been lying to you.

JEAN-JACQUES *(after a moment)* When?

SUZANNE I haven't found a flat. It's all a lie. I haven't even looked for one. I made it all up. I never meant to go away.

JEAN-JACQUES Don't waste your breath.

SUZANNE It's true.

JEAN-JACQUES I don't believe you any longer.

SUZANNE . I swear I'm telling you the truth now.

JEAN-JACQUES Why did you leave this morning?

SUZANNE To get cigarettes.

JEAN-JACQUES What about the man from the agency?

SUZANNE He doesn't exist.

JEAN-JACQUES And the horn...?

SUZANNE A passing car.

JEAN-JACQUES It's not true.

SUZANNE *(moved)* Yes it is. The proof is that I'm staying here. You see? I'm staying. Nobody's expecting me in the street. And this splendid terrace, I've never seen it. I invented it. *(She sits down.)* What got into you? All that shouting, these stupid whims? Why? You've known hundreds of women, but the mere idea of my leaving turns your whole world upside down.

JEAN-JACQUES   Don't exaggerate.

SUZANNE   Don't be so gullible.

JEAN-JACQUES   I believe what I'm told.

SUZANNE   You must calm down. You force me to play disgraceful tricks! Show me your normal face again. You will go to work later on.

JEAN-JACQUES   You won't leave?

SUZANNE   No.

JEAN-JACQUES   You'll stay here?

SUZANNE   Yes.

JEAN-JACQUES   How long?

SUZANNE   For a while, yes. If you stay cool. Otherwise I'll leave.

JEAN-JACQUES   What about our marriage?

SUZANNE   Out of the question.

JEAN-JACQUES   Why?

SUZANNE   I don't want to.

JEAN-JACQUES   You're married already?

SUZANNE   Shush ! No more questions, remember. I've told you already, I'm not in the mood for marriage. The idea simply disgusts me. I think I'd just die.

JEAN-JACQUES   I see.

SUZANNE   Go to work.

JEAN-JACQUES   Tomorrow. Please spare me a few hours. Don't throw me out. Let me stay here with you, this afternoon, and this evening.

SUZANNE   You take things too much to heart. What am I to do with you?

JEAN-JACQUES   May I stay?

SUZANNE It is your flat. That makes it hard for me to throw you out… Maybe I should leave, in any case.

She stands up and moves two steps away.

JEAN-JACQUES You're mad. Come and sit next to me. *(He smiles at her and holds out his hand to her.)* I feel much better. I can see things clearly again.
SUZANNE *(on her guard)* Now I find it hard to believe you.
JEAN-JACQUES Come and sit here, I feel so good.

She doesn't move.

JEAN-JACQUES Don't be scared. Please.
SUZANNE *(sitting down again)* I shouldn't. But I feel so weak in front of you. It's true. I had such a hard time lying to you. Promise me you'll go to the office later on, if I sit down.
JEAN-JACQUES I'm not making any promises.
SUZANNE If that's what you want.

She moves close to him, keeping a certain reserve.

JEAN-JACQUES You've won. Let's enjoy the moment. You're here, I'm happy, very well. You're not here, I'm crying, too bad. I'll do everything you want. Absolutely everything. *(pause. He looks at her and asks smiling.)* Try me, right now – what would you like me to do?
SUZANNE Go to the office.

He stands up, takes his hat and leaves straight away.
Lights fade.

SCENE 6

Suzanne is alone in the flat, carefully reading the little black book. She leafs through the pages slowly, goes backwards… Suddenly she lifts her head and looks towards the door as if she'd heard a noise. False alarm. She gets up, glances through the window, then checks the time on her alarm clock. Coming back to the little black book she picks up a magazine. (Many magazines are still scattered on the floor.) Noticing her mistake, she throws the magazine on the floor, takes the little black book and abandons herself to it. She has her back towards the entrance door. At that moment Jean-Jacques opens the door and walks in without a sound. She doesn't notice him. He silently shuts the door and looks at Suzanne with a smile. He is carelessly holding a black attaché case. It is as though Suzanne hadn't heard him… yet.

SUZANNE   You're back late.
JEAN-JACQUES   I had lots of things to do, sorry. *(He kisses her on the forehead.)* Good evening.
SUZANNE   Good evening.

In a corner of the flat, there is a large suitcase, closed.

JEAN-JACQUES   Were you waiting for me?
SUZANNE   I was waiting for you, indeed I was. And would you believe it, time dragged.
JEAN-JACQUES   It won't happen again.
SUZANNE   Don't apologise. After all, that's how it should be. What time do you usually get home?

He doesn't answer and points to the suitcase.

JEAN-JACQUES   Is that mine?

SUZANNE   What?

JEAN-JACQUES   That suitcase.

SUZANNE   Yes I took it out of the cupboard and
put mine in. You suggested it, remember?

JEAN-JACQUES   Of course I remember.

He catches a glimpse of the raincoat.

SUZANNE   I had to make some room. If we're
going to be living together, we'll need every bit of space.
So I got rid of all your old suits and a few pairs of shoes
with pointy toes. Men have this thing about their old
clothes, it's ridiculous. I put them all in your suitcase.

JEAN-JACQUES   You did very well.

SUZANNE   So you don't mind?

JEAN-JACQUES   Oh no.

SUZANNE   I actually think you should throw
away this suitcase.

JEAN-JACQUES   I will, tomorrow or the day after. *(He
points to the raincoat on the bed and asks absent-
mindedly.)* What's that?

SUZANNE   What's what?

JEAN-JACQUES   That.

She hesitates for a moment.

SUZANNE *(without looking at Jean-Jacques)* Monsieur
Ferrand came this afternoon. He left his raincoat.

*A pause. She spies on Jean-Jacques' reactions. He neither
looks surprised nor angry. He takes the raincoat and holds it
up at arm's length.*

JEAN-JACQUES	That's a nice raincoat, brand new.
SUZANNE	Ah.
JEAN-JACQUES	Very good quality too.

He goes in front of the wardrobe mirror and calmly puts on the raincoat. It is ridiculously too large for him. It falls down to his ankles and the sleeves cover his hands completely.

SUZANNE	It doesn't suit you very well.
JEAN-JACQUES	Doesn't it?
SUZANNE	No.
JEAN-JACQUES	You may be right. Usually I have trouble seeing what suits me and what doesn't, but in this case…
SUZANNE	Yes.
JEAN-JACQUES	I'll take it off.

He takes it off and holds it up at arm's length.

SUZANNE Doesn't surprise me. Monsieur Ferrand is much taller and much broader than you. He is a giant.

JEAN-JACQUES He must be.

SUZANNE *(slightly hesitating).* He stayed here… at least three hours… It was already dusk when he left… There was so much we had to say to each other, after so long…

Seeing that Jean-Jacques has folded the raincoat and is nonchalantly throwing it out of the window, she stops talking. Jean-Jacques then calmly shuts the window and fetches two glasses and a bottle. Suzanne watches him.

JEAN-JACQUES Would you care for a drink?

SUZANNE *(stunned)* Why did you throw it out?

JEAN-JACQUES   The raincoat?

SUZANNE   Yes.

JEAN-JACQUES   Because it didn't suit me.

SUZANNE   What if Monsieur Ferrand comes back for it?

JEAN-JACQUES *(handling her a glass)* That's your problem. *(He raises his glass.)* Cheers. *(He drinks. She follows.)* You were just telling me the flat was too small. I wasn't going to bother with that monstrous raincoat. *(He takes a few steps.)* Now that I think about it, I could throw a lot of things out of the window. *(His eyes stop on her.)* Almost everything.

SUZANNE   There's no hurry.

JEAN-JACQUES   I wonder.

Suzanne tries to regain confidence and resume her story. Jean-Jacques goes from one object to the other, wondering. He looks at her gravely.

SUZANNE   In the end it was what I thought. He'd given me the wrong address. He didn't do it on purpose though. Well, so he says.

JEAN-JACQUES   Who?

SUZANNE   Monsieur Ferrand. There's no reason why I shouldn't believe him. And when he finally realised, he returned… thinner… whiter…

JEAN-JACQUES   Anything left to eat?

SUZANNE   Are you hungry?

JEAN-JACQUES   Yes.

He goes to the kitchen to get something to eat.

SUZANNE   You'll find everything I bought yesterday and the day before. Apart from a few biscuits and tea bags. With your permission I offered Monsieur Ferrand some tea. Of course he made it. I did wash the cups though.

JEAN-JACQUES *(coming back)* Congratulations.

He carries on behaving the same way, letting Suzanne get more lost in her awkward explanations. From time to time he nods at what she is saying.

SUZANNE   From what I could make out, he came to have me back. He blamed himself for everything… Now he's free… It's a long story you know, Jean-Jacques… One of those never-ending stories… very common when you think of it… *(Jean-Jacques nods his head but doesn't say anything.)* He was very calm… not nearly as passionate as he used to be… but still with that powerful sense of comfort and understanding.

JEAN-JACQUES   Shall we have dinner and go to the cinema or go to the cinema and then have dinner?

SUZANNE   Are you not interested?

JEAN-JACQUES   I'm sorry?

SUZANNE   About what I'm telling you!

JEAN-JACQUES   Whatever you say is interesting to me.

SUZANNE   So you could at least listen to me.

JEAN-JACQUES *(lying down in front of her)* I'm all ears. Carry on.

SUZANNE   I'd rather not say anything.

JEAN-JACQUES   For a change.

SUZANNE   Yes, for a change, thank you.

JEAN-JACQUES   You won't keep to that for more than a minute.

SUZANNE   You want to bet?

JEAN-JACQUES   Usually, you don't need to be begged to start talking. Words tend to flow out of your mouth. But today, honestly I don't recognise you... What's the matter with you? What you're saying doesn't make sense... You seem to be talking randomly, awkwardly, with something else on your mind...

SUZANNE *(in a low voice)* Yes.

JEAN-JACQUES *(after a while)* You didn't keep to it.

SUZANNE   We haven't even started yet.

An awkward moment. Jean-Jacques looks away and sees the little black book in Suzanne's hands.

JEAN-JACQUES   You're still reading it?

SUZANNE   I'm learning it by heart.

JEAN-JACQUES   That's an idea!

SUZANNE   It's practically the only way I've found to learn things about you.

JEAN-JACQUES   About me?

SUZANNE   Yes. *(irritated)* I should at least know you a little, shouldn't I?

JEAN-JACQUES   Now what are you talking about? You know me perfectly well! I've been very honest with you! I've held nothing back from you! Which is more than you can say!

SUZANNE   You are absolutely extraordinary! *(vividly)* You haven't got the faintest idea! It's the other way round! I don't know anything about you! You keep on questioning me. You know I love it. And you stand there, staring at me, silently. But you? What about you? Who are you? *(For the first time she seems to be completely lost, very worried. She shows him the little black book.)* So when you're away, I try to learn more about you, through the things you like.

JEAN-JACQUES   I've changed a lot.

SUZANNE   Think of me! I haven't a clue what's the matter with me and I don't like that. My feelings are all over the place.

JEAN-JACQUES   It will pass.

SUZANNE   I don't think so. No, I really don't think so. Do you remember how flustered I was when I arrived yesterday morning?

JEAN-JACQUES   Flustered?

SUZANNE   Yes, flustered, confused, completely lost. Do you remember?

JEAN-JACQUES   Yes, maybe…

SUZANNE   You must admit that things have changed.

JEAN-JACQUES   I can't see…

SUZANNE   You can't see because you can't face things! I was so much hoping for a peaceful break… To get some strength together before leaving… And now I don't even know where I am… I make up ridiculous stories… I can't find anything better than to buy raincoats… No wonder you end up mocking me… I've no energy left, no spirit… I sit here, waiting for you… If you're late, I worry… I walk round and round thinking about you… And yet I don't even know you! I don't know you at all!

As Jean-Jacques listens, he becomes increasingly surprised, and happy.

JEAN-JACQUES   Suzanne, you're not serious, are you?

SUZANNE   Of course I am! What do I know about you? Tell me? I vaguely know about your job, so little really! Then what? I know your first name and that's all! That's all! I don't even know your last name!

She stands up to put the notebook back into the bookshelf. He says artlessly without looking at her.

JEAN-JACQUES   My name is Ferrand. Jean-Jacques
  Ferrand.

He turns to her. She looks at him stunned.
Lights fade.

SCENE 7

The next morning. Jean-Jacques and Suzanne are sitting opposite each other, having breakfast. He has finished while she is still carefully eating and drinking. As she finishes every single bite, they remain silent. They smile at each other, they seem happy. Suzanne looks away first. She examines the flat.

SUZANNE   I have a few ideas for the decoration. I'll tell you as soon as we have time.

JEAN-JACQUES   Whatever you want.

She goes into the bathroom to fetch a jacket and brings it to Jean-Jacques.

SUZANNE   Your jacket.

JEAN-JACQUES   Thank you

He takes the jacket but instead of putting it on, he throws it on a chair. Slightly embarrassed, she sits opposite him. They remain silent for a while. She takes a magazine and leafs through it. Then she asks Jean-Jacques.

SUZANNE   What time is it?

JEAN-JACQUES *(smiling)* I don't know.

SUZANNE   Don't you have a watch?

JEAN-JACQUES   It stopped two days ago. Check your alarm clock.

SUZANNE   Oh yes. *(She gets up and checks.)* It's five to nine. You're going to be late.

JEAN-JACQUES   No I'm not.

SUZANNE   Don't you have meetings this morning?

JEAN-JACQUES   No.

SUZANNE	What about the Bugeot will?
JEAN-JACQUES	Done and dusted.

Silence. She sits opposite him again. After a brief moment.

SUZANNE.	You're not going to work?
JEAN-JACQUES	No. Not this morning.
SUZANNE	You're staying here?
JEAN-JACQUES	Yes.
SUZANNE	And… this afternoon?
JEAN-JACQUES	This afternoon too.
SUZANNE	So… you are staying here all day?
JEAN-JACQUES	Yes.

SUZANNE   You'll go for a stroll though, it'll do you good.

JEAN-JACQUES   Absolutely not.

SUZANNE   But what about your practice? Your job? *(He waves his hand airily.)* What's that supposed to mean?

JEAN-JACQUES *(always smiling)* You won't be able to put my work down anymore.

SUZANNE   I never did that!

JEAN-JACQUES   Yes you did…

SUZANNE   Hardly… *(She stands up to take the breakfast tray back to the kitchen.)*

JEAN-JACQUES   I sold my half to Michel.

SUZANNE *(from the kitchen)* What?

JEAN-JACQUES   My half of the partnership; I sold it to Michel.

SUZANNE *(returning)* When?

JEAN-JACQUES   Yesterday afternoon.

SUZANNE   Yesterday afternoon?

JEAN-JACQUES Yes. That's why I was late. Working out the details.

SUZANNE Why didn't you tell me?

JEAN-JACQUES We had other things to talk about.

SUZANNE Really? So it's all over?

JEAN-JACQUES Business is over. Over. The selling, the buying, the will. And the old lady. And the Registration, the companies, the ownership, the fees. All done with! *(pause)* I sold all my shares to Michel for a song. He seemed rather glad.

SUZANNE What are you going to do?

JEAN-JACQUES When?

SUZANNE From now on?

JEAN-JACQUES *(happily)* Lots of things. *(Suzanne looks at him questioningly.)* First I'm going to lock the door. *(He does and then paces about the flat. Suzanne stands to watch him).* Tomorrow, I'm going to barricade it. I've got ideas for the decoration too. And I'm going to have some peace and quiet! I'm going to follow your advice. I'm going to sound proof the walls and the ceilings. No more cracks, no more holes. Cramps, insulators, glass wool, everywhere. Some tar as well. *(He points to the TV.)* We'll breed goldfish in there. When we get hungry we'll eat them. *(He strides to the bookshelf.)* I shall burn my books and my shelves. I shall give my CD's to the poor. *(The phone rings. He rips out the connection.)* Cut off everything! We don't need all this noise any longer. The doorbell too. *(He pulls out the wires.)* There. We are completely shut off from everything. And that's only the beginning! The next step is to stock up enough food and drink for an indefinite period of time, and cigarettes, and magazines. We'll set the thermostat to an invariable temperature and live by electric light. We'll close the curtains forever. I won't hear about daylight anymore. I won't have draughts. I won't stand creaking floors or knocks on the

walls. I don't ever want to know whether it's winter or
summer, day or night.

SUZANNE	It's past nine o'clock, in the morning!
JEAN-JACQUES	Be quiet! *(now a long silence)*
JEAN-JACQUES	Why aren't you saying anything?
SUZANNE	You told me to keep quiet.
JEAN-JACQUES	That's no reason.
SUZANNE	Yes it is.
JEAN-JACQUES	Don't be so obedient.
SUZANNE	Don't complain.

JEAN-JACQUES   Who's complaining? We're alive.
We're together. All my wishes are coming true. *(pause)*
Suzanne, what do you think of my decision? Are you
surprised?

SUZANNE   Yes, somehow I am.

JEAN-JACQUES   You must be. It certainly surprised
Michel. And me too actually. I still can't get over it.

SUZANNE   Aren't you ever going to work again?

JEAN-JACQUES   Never. Ever.

SUZANNE   And you're going to be here. Night
and day. With me.

JEAN-JACQUES   Isn't that what you wanted?

SUZANNE   I don't know what I want.

He sits opposite her and says in a gentle voice:

JEAN-JACQUES   To start with you made me late,
several times in one day. Remember… After that you
talked about me, my job, the way I live. How many times
did you tell me – I hate work, nobody should have to work.
Isn't that true? *(She nods.)* And I said to myself: She's
right! She's totally right. Suddenly, it was all clear! I would
never go to work again. I would never be late again

because I'd never have anything to be on time for. I 'll be here. My hours will be yours.

SUZANNE   Mine?

JEAN-JACQUES   Yes.

SUZANNE   What for?

A pause, he is slightly perplexed.

JEAN-JACQUES   Yesterday, or the day before, I can't remember anymore, you told me: "I'm at your disposal" You did, didn't you? *(She nods.)* Today, it's my turn. I'm all yours Suzanne – to do whatever you want.

SUZANNE   I am… embarrassed.

JEAN-JACQUES   Embarrassed? I thought you'd be over the moon!

SUZANNE   Let me get used to the idea.

JEAN-JACQUES   Take your time, please.

SUZANNE   You seem so extreme all a sudden!

JEAN-JACQUES   That's how I felt yesterday evening. Now I'm all right.

He sits next to her.

SUZANNE   Jean-Jacques, put yourself in my position. I never expected anything like this from you. It's not that I don't care about you, far from it. *(She takes his arm.)* I can't say why but the idea of having you always around, bothers me. Always always here. Only for me. Is it really necessary?

JEAN-JACQUES   Was it too hasty?

SUZANNE   Maybe.

JEAN-JACQUES   I can't tell.

SUZANNE   It's all a joke?

JEAN-JACQUES   What kind of a joke?

SUZANNE *(laughing)* You're pulling my leg. You haven't sold Michel a thing! Just because I teased you with that story about my flat, you have to get even with me. That's what it's all about.

JEAN-JACQUES   I did sell everything.

SUZANNE   I don't believe you.

JEAN-JACQUES   I swear.

An awkward moment. She turns away.

SUZANNE   Well, after all. It's your business, not mine. I've no idea… Women shouldn't meddle in such matters anyway. So what do we do now?

JEAN-JACQUES   How about a cup of coffee?

SUZANNE *(abruptly)* Call Michel this minute! Tell him you're not selling, it was all a joke. You lost your head and you'll be there tomorrow as usual.

JEAN-JACQUES   Too late.

SUZANNE   He wouldn't refuse?

JEAN-JACQUES   Who cares what he would do? I refuse.

SUZANNE   Don't be so stubborn. You're too young to be doing nothing. That's what my grandfather used to say, even to very old people.

JEAN-JACQUES   When did he retire?

SUZANNE   When he died.

JEAN-JACQUES   What did he die of?

SUZANNE   None of your business.

JEAN-JACQUES   I don't have an ounce of respect for your grandfather.

SUZANNE   Neither do I. But he was my grandfather.

JEAN-JACQUES   As of this afternoon, I have reached the right age for doing nothing.

SUZANNE   Idleness is the mother of all vice.

JEAN-JACQUES   You're the right one to say that!

SUZANNE   Day after day in this place for the rest of your life, what will you do?

JEAN-JACQUES   Who'd know better than you?

SUZANNE   This is all my fault, and it probably seems like I pressured you into it. I understand why you feel that way. You took me word for word when I always say the first thing that comes into my head. You know Jean-Jacques, when you were away, I wanted to see you. Truly. And the more you were away, the more I wanted to see you… but now the idea that you'll never leave again… well, already I can't stand you any longer. Remember what you wanted so much, now you'll get it. I'll leave. I'll run away no matter what you try to do. You'll see. One day you'll be careless, maybe you'll sleep too late in the morning, and when you get up, I'll be gone... Believe me, it will break my heart.

JEAN-JACQUES   What about your suitcase?

SUZANNE   I'll leave it as my sacrifice – my dresses, my books, my alarm clock, all yours in memory of me. I'll go completely naked if I must, but I'll go.

JEAN-JACQUES   All my shares are sold. I'll never see Michel again.

SUZANNE (*repeating in a low voice*) I shall go.
(*Silence. They are sitting next to each other. Jean-Jacques stands up, calm and determined. He takes his jacket and puts it on.*) What are you doing?

JEAN-JACQUES   I'm leaving.

SUZANNE   Leaving?

JEAN-JACQUES   Yes.

SUZANNE   For the office?

JEAN-JACQUES   No.

SUZANNE   So where are you going?

JEAN-JACQUES   I have a feeling you like this place.
You can have it. *(She is stunned. He adds in a calm voice.)*
I'll live somewhere else, anywhere. It doesn't matter to me.
I don't care. I'm not scared of hotels.

SUZANNE   I beg your pardon?

He takes his suitcase and gives his last words of advice.

JEAN-JACQUES   Lock the door after me. And take it
easy. The phone's cut off, nobody will bother you. I'll tell
the concierge not to let anybody up. Not even a blind man.
(He shows her his key.) I'm keeping a key. I'll come and
see you from time to time.

SUZANNE   When?

JEAN-JACQUES   From time to time. Quite often, I
imagine.

SUZANNE   Will you let me know before?

JEAN-JACQUES   No, if that's all right.

SUZANNE   What if you don't come back?

JEAN-JACQUES *(looking at her, sure of himself)* I'll be
back. I promise you that I'll be back.

SUZANNE   What if I'm not here?

JEAN-JACQUES   I think you'll be here…

SUZANNE   What if I decide to leave?

JEAN-JACQUES   You won't leave. Not yet at least. You
like it here. Lie down, relax. Wait for me. You have
everything you need? You know about the heating?

She nods. She understands him and approves.

SUZANNE   I'll manage.

JEAN-JACQUES	How are you for money?
SUZANNE	I have some left.
JEAN-JACQUES over there.	There's another key in the drawer,
SUZANNE	Thank you.
JEAN-JACQUES	See if you want to keep the cleaning

woman. She knows the place. She won't get in the way.

SUZANNE	Very well.

He walks to the door, she follows him with her eyes.

JEAN-JACQUES while.	Oh, do water the plants, once in a
SUZANNE	What about your mail?
JEAN-JACQUES when I come by.	There'll be less and less. I'll pick it up
SUZANNE	And your little black book?
JEAN-JACQUES	It's yours. *(He tries to open the door and pulls several times because it is locked, before unlocking it. As he walks out:)* See you soon…

She stares at the door. She walks up and down, unsettled, helpless. She turns on the music. The same record. She sits on the bed. She looks at the door once more.
She is motionless.
Lights fade.

The end.

ORDER FORM

- LYSISTRATA- THE SEX STRIKE BY GERMAINE GREER £7.99
- DEVOTION BY LEO BUTLER £7.99
- UNDER THEIR INFLUENCE BY WAYNE BUCHANAN £6.99
- THREE PLAYS BY JONATHAN MOORE £10.95
- THE CLASSIC FAIRYTALES (RETOLD FOR THE STAGE) £11.50
- BLACK AND ASIAN PLAYS ANTHOLOGY £9.95
- SEVEN PLAYS BY WOMEN £5.95
- SIX PLAYS BY BLACK AND ASIAN WOMEN £7.50
- MEDITERRANEAN PLAYS BY WOMEN £9.95
- A TOUCH OF THE DUTCH £9.95
- YOUNG BLOOD, PLAYS FOR YOUNG PERFORMERS £10.95
- CHARLES WAY, PLAYS FOR YOUNG PEOPLE £9.95
- BEST OF THE FEST £12.99
- EASTERN PROMISE £11.99
- BALKAN PLOTS £9.95
- HOW MAXINE LEARNED TO LOVE HER LEGS £8.95
- SACRED BY ELIETTE ABECASSIS £9.95

ADD 10% UK / 20% INTERNATIONAL POST AND PACKING

NAME _____

ADDRESS_____

_____

_____

POSTCODE _____

PAYMENT BY CHEQUE OR POSTAL ORDER IN £ STERLING TO:
AURORA METRO PRESS
4 OSIER MEWS, LONDON W4 2NT. UK.
TEL. +44 (0) 208 747 1953   www.aurorametro.com